Critics, Monsters, Fanatics,
and Other Literary Essays

Also by Cynthia Ozick

CRITICS, MONSTERS, FANATICS, AND OTHER LITERARY ESSAYS

CYNTHIA OZICK

Houghton Mifflin Harcourt

BOSTON   NEW YORK

2016

For information about permission to reproduce selections from this book,
write to trade.permissions@hmhco.com or to
Permissions, Houghton Mifflin Harcourt Publishing Company,
3 Park Avenue, 19th Floor, New York, New York 10016.

www.hmhco.com

Library of Congress Cataloging-in-Publication Data
Names: Ozick, Cynthia, author.
Title: Critics, monsters, fanatics, and other literary essays / Cynthia Ozick.
Description: Boston : Houghton Mifflin Harcourt, 2016.
Identifiers: LCCN 2015037560 | ISBN 9780544703711 (hardback) | ISBN
9780544703698 (ebook)
Subjects: LCSH: Criticism. | BISAC: LITERARY CRITICISM / Books & Reading. |
LITERARY CRITICISM / American / General.
Classification: LCC PN81.O95 2016 | DDC 801/.95 — dc23
LC record available at http://lccn.loc.gov/2015037560

Book design by Mark Robinson

Printed in the United States of America
DOC 10 9 8 7 6 5 4 3 2 1

Essays in this book originally appeared, in different form, in the following: "Out from
Xanadu," "I Write Because I Hate," "Please, Stories Are Stories," "An Empty Coffin,"
and "The Rhapsodist," in the *New York Times Book Review;* "Writers, Visible and
Invisible" in *PEN Magazine* and *Standpoint* (UK); "The Boys in the Alley,
the Disappearing Readers, and the Novel's Ghostly Twin" in *Harper's Magazine;*
"W. H. Auden at the 92nd Street Y" in the *Paris Review Online;* and "The Lastingness
of Saul Bellow," "Nobility Eclipsed," "Transcending the Kafkaesque," "Love and Levity
at Auschwitz," and "Novel or Nothing" in the *New Republic.*

Permissions credits appear on page 213.

For
L. W.,
inspiriter

Authors are partial to their Wit, 'tis true.

But are not Criticks to their Judgment too?

... Those monsters, Criticks!

— ALEXANDER POPE,
"An Essay on Criticism," 1711

Contents

Critics

GEORGE ORWELL AND EDMUND WILSON ARE emblematic names that have come down to us from the still ticking heart of the twentieth century—literary names that carry *meaning*. Speak of Orwell, and what reverberates is monitory: *Animal Farm* and *1984*, each a forceful parable of totalitarian oppression. But Orwell was also renowned as a sonorous essayist, one who is nowadays not much read beyond the campus, where "Shooting an Elephant" is a mainstay of the college anthologies. Except for *Animal Farm*, his fiction fails to attract ongoing notice—least of all *Keep the Aspidistra Flying*, long ago interred among the forgotten social novels of the 1930s. And apart from Orwell specialists, who now reads *The Road to Wigan Pier*? Yet *Big Brother* and *Newspeak* and *memory hole* are so ingrained in the common idiom that for many it hardly seems necessary to trouble to turn the already familiar pages of *1984*. None of this matters; what counts is the echo of Orwell's name and the bleakness it evokes: dread; deception; injustice; anomie; soullessness. Orwell has become Orwellian.

Edmund Wilson germinates no parallel verbal progeny: Wilsonian, if it suggests anything, characterizes the policies of an American president. We have no single term — no summarizing atmospheric word — for America's preeminent critic, who has no peer and may never be surpassed. He encompassed worlds: he wrote on the Iroquois, on an ancient Hebrew religious sect, on Russian philology, on the French Symbolists, on the evolution of radical political movements from Robespierre to the Bolsheviks, on the Civil War; he wrote on Canada and on Haiti, on citizenship and taxation, on movies and theater, on poets and novelists, on historical figures and on his contemporaries. He also wrote — critically — on literary criticism.

In 1928, in an acerbic and dismissive essay titled "The Critic Who Does Not Exist," he complained of the lack of serious literary criticism in the United States. "A work of art," he said, "is not a set of ideas or an exercise of technique, or even a combination of both. But I am strongly disposed to believe that our contemporary writing would benefit by a genuine literary criticism that should deal expertly with ideas and art. . . . In a sense, it can probably be said that no such creature exists as a full-time literary critic — that is, a writer who is at once first-rate and nothing but a literary critic." Wilson, of course, *was* that creature, and today there are a number of first-rate writers of criticism who are at work full-time; but are there enough to make what can be called an expansive literary culture?

If we isolate only one decade of the many Wilson dominated — the 1920s, say — the extent and variety of his perceptions and preoccupations astonish. It is as if Wilson were not one critic but scores of critics, all working separately in their respective specialties. His "All-Star Literary Vaudeville" is an essay that ranges over dozens of writers, most of them durably familiar to their posterity — Dreiser, Mencken, Willa Cather, Sherwood Anderson — though some, like Carl Van Vechten and Joseph Hergesheimer, today seem no more visible than distant ghosts. Between 1924 and 1928 alone, Wilson rounded up his reflections on Houdini, Poe, dialect and slang, e. e. cummings, Woodrow Wilson's years at Princeton, Ring Lardner, Eugene O'Neill, Hemingway, F. Scott Fitzgerald, Byron's mistresses, subjects such as "the humility of common sense" and "the trouble with American comedy," John Dos Passos, T. S. Eliot, Ezra Pound, Henry James, Upton Sinclair, a Prohibition-era speakeasy; and much more, all in seamlessly lucid prose.

It should be understood — it should be trumpeted — that not one of these essays is dated. Not one is infected by staleness. Wilson's achievement rises beyond reviewing, giving the news, assessing his time. Read him now and see the lineaments of a civilization; he reproduces nothing less. The critic has become a historian.

And here is the shock of it. Wilson stands as a kind of symbol — far more than a literary model to aspire to. He is what current lingo, falling into the tedium of overuse, terms an "icon," the embodiment of an indissoluble fame. And like Orwell, whose repute — whose meaning — is similarly enduring, *he is not read.* Admired, honored, influential, legendary; rumored, but not read. Which brings us, alarmingly, to the

Orwellian: the dying of the imagination through the invisibility of the past. As for the uses of criticism by the denizens of the present moment: envisioning society whole by way of the contemplation of its parts, the delicate along with the tumultuous, the weighty together with the trifling, is how a culture can learn to imagine its own face.

Without the critics, incoherence.

The Boys in the Alley, the Disappearing Readers, and the Novel's Ghostly Twin

"On or about December 1910," Virginia Woolf wrote more than one hundred years ago, "human character changed." The phrase has come down to us mockingly, notoriously, but also with the truth-like endurance of a maxim. By a change in human character, Woolf meant modernism, and by modernism she meant the kind of overt self-consciousness that identifies and interrogates its own motions and motives. Set forth in "Character in Fiction," an essay arguing for innovation in the novel, it was an aesthetic rather than an essentialist proposition. The change—a new dispensation of premise and utterance—had been wickedly heralded two years before, on an August afternoon in 1908, when Lytton Strachey happened to notice a stain on Woolf's sister's skirt. "Semen?" Strachey inquired, as definitively as the final squeal of a hinge: a door flung shut for the last time. Behind that door lurked the muzzled premodern, and before it swarmed what modernism has long since made of us (and postmodernism even more so): harriers of the hour, sooth-sayers and pulse-takers, augurs and dowsers, examiners of entrails. Literary entrails especially: many are the stains subject to writerly divination.

And so it was that on or about April 1996, Jonathan Franzen published a manifesto on the situation of the contemporary novelist (with himself as chief specimen and proof text), and the character of bookish querulousness changed. What had been muttered mutely in cenacles and bars erupted uninhibitedly in print, as flagrante delicto as any old spot of early-twentieth-century semen. *The Corrections,* Franzen's ambitious and celebrated literary bestseller, had not yet appeared; he was still a mostly obscure fiction writer whose two previous novels, though praised by reviewers, had slid into the usual quicksand of forgotten books. When a little-known writer undertakes a manifesto—a statement, after all, of sober purpose and principle—it is likely also to be a cri de coeur, and its reasoned argument will derive from the intimate wounds of autobiography. "I'd intended to provoke; what I got instead," Franzen said of his first novel, "was sixty reviews in a vacuum." Even sixty reviews, he made plain, was not sufficient: it was not equivalent to a public event, attention was not being paid, certainly not in the coin of genuine Fame, and the vacuum in question was the airlessness of writer's depression.

It was a brave stand, then, to issue a manifesto in the form of a turbulent confluence of introspective memoir and cultural analysis; nor was it a career move, despite its publication in a major magazine. Literary essays are generally well beneath popular notice, and Franzen's piece, though pumped up by anecdote ("When I got off the phone, I couldn't stop laughing") and political apocalypse ("the United States seemed to me . . . terminally out of touch with reality"), aroused its expected flurry among the literati, but was overlooked by Oprah. It took *The Corrections* to catch the eye, and then the ire, of television's latter-day publishing goddess, and Franzen's fame was confirmed. Retrospectively, if the success of *The Corrections* had not catapulted Franzen into precisely those precincts of the literary stratosphere he had so ringingly and publicly coveted, his declaration might have disintegrated, like all other articles of passing faith, into a half-remembered bleat.

This has not happened—partly because Franzen continues as a noted writerly presence, and partly because his observations of nearly twenty years ago have failed to escape the transience of mere personal complaint. There were many such ventings, embedded in irritating and by now obsolete trivia, to wit: ". . . even as I was sanctifying the reading of literature, I was becoming so depressed that I could do little after dinner but flop in front of the TV. Even without cable, I could always find something delicious: Phillies and Padres, Eagles and Bengals, *M*A*S*H, Cheers, Homicide*." Still more grumbling followed, about the discouraging fate of a second novel: "But the result was the same: another report card with A's and B's from the reviewers who had replaced the teachers whose approval, when I was younger, I had both craved and taken no satisfaction from; decent sales; and the deafening silence of irrelevance"—all this as if private grievance could rise to societal position-taking. Yet the deafening silence of irrelevance was, finally, the undergirding of Franzen's point: that the common culture has undermined the novelist's traditional role as newsbringer. Novelists, he said, "do feel a responsibility to dramatize important issues of the day, and they now confront a culture in which almost all the issues are burned out almost all of the time." They are burned out by the proliferating, instantaneous, and superior technological sources of what Franzen calls "social instruction."

His subject, in short, was the decline of reading in an electronic age when scores of plots, shocks, titillations, and unfolding dramatic disclosures, shot out daily by the reality machines of radio, television, the Internet, endlessly evolving apps, and the journalist's confiding up-to-the-nanosecond cell phone and Twitter appear to supply all the storytelling seductions anyone might thirst after. Franzen was hardly the first writer to notice this; he acknowledged that Philip Roth, three decades earlier, was already despairing of the novel's viability in the face of mad actuality's pervasive power. Franzen's thesis was not fresh, but neither was it stale. What *was* new was his linking the question of public literacy with marketplace lust, with — in an idiom Norman Podhoretz made famous nearly forty years ago — Making It. Having confessed to a blatant desire for success ("the dirty little secret"), Podhoretz was roundly excoriated, so much so that if flogging had been legal, the reigning literary-intellectual tribe of that period would have come after him with a forest of cat-o'-nine-tails. It was a time, moreover, when the publication of a serious literary novel was an exuberant communal event; only recall how *The Naked and the Dead,* or *The Adventures of Augie March,* was received. And it was a time, paradoxically, when serious writers looked down on the wider publishing marketplace and were sedulously detached from it: "popular" novelists were scorned. No one spoke of the decline of reading because it had not yet occurred.

All that is nowadays extinct. Ambition, even of the kind termed naked, no longer invites elitist denunciation. Writers who define themselves by the loftiest standards of literary art are happy to be counted as popular; the lucky ones gratefully, not to say covetously, accept the high advances that signify the hope for a six-digit readership. But fifty years ago, Lionel Trilling, the paramount critic of the American midcentury, inveighed against the democratic wider audience, and the "big advertising appropriation" that accompanied it, as corrupting forces — even as he worshiped Hemingway, who had the largest readership of any serious novelist then writing. In an essay titled "The Function of the Little Magazine" (referring to the literary quarterlies that once occupied the pinnacle of intellectual prestige), Trilling recommended, and extolled, the most ideal readership of all, no matter how closed or small or invisible or abstract or imaginary. "The writer must define his audience by its abilities, by its perfections," he insisted. "He does well, if he cannot see his right audience within immediate reach of his voice, to direct his words to his spiritual ancestors, or to posterity, or even, if need be, to a coterie."

A coterie! Spiritual ancestors! Posterity! Such martyred satisfactions are a long way from Franzen's appetite, or the appetite of his contemporaries. Trilling demanded a self-denying purity; purity for the sake of a higher purity. Franzen, more pragmatic and businesslike, talks numbers. "The educated single New Yorker who in 1945 read twenty-five serious novels in a year today has time for maybe five," he writes. "That hard core is a very small prize to be divided among a very large number of working novelists," and he tots up the few who, back in 1996, "actually hit the charts": "Annie Proulx's *The Shipping News* has sold nearly a million copies in the last two years; the hardcover literary best-seller *The Crossing,* by Cormac McCarthy, came in on the *Publishers Weekly* annual best-seller list." (Up there in Paradise, among his spiritual ancestors, one can hear Trilling's fastidious sighs.) By now, Franzen has caught up with, or perhaps surpassed, those impressive sales figures of twenty years ago. And if Trilling cannot be Franzen's spiritual ancestor (he once tried out the purity path, he tells us), it is because our world has left reticence behind: a reticence that, for Franzen, has come to resemble "an estrangement from humanity." He calls it that; but what he *means* is being "known," and escape from the confinements of a small readership, and finally that desirable state, or trait, that goes by the name of "accessibility." All the same, the terminology of publishing success has grown softer with the years. Instead of the brash Making It, there is the melancholy worry over the silence of irrelevance. Almost no one, least of all Franzen, is asking for invisible, unheard coteries.

Yet in October of 2005 Trilling (or his proselytizing shade) made an unexpected comeback, in the form of an answering manifesto that challenged Franzen's. Under a gaudy banner — "Why Experimental Fiction Threatens to Destroy Publishing, Jonathan Franzen, and Life as We Know It," slyly subtitled "A Correction" — Ben Marcus, Franzen's dedicated antagonist, undertook, Trilling-like, to prescribe the nature of his ideal reader. Marcus's reader was not Franzen's. Franzen had identified the born reader as a "social isolate" in childhood, an insight supplied to him by a practicing sociologist. Marcus's own definition was derived from the fairy realm of elixirs and transmutations. "A writer might be forgiven," he said, "for wishing to slip readers enhancements to their Wernicke's areas [the segment of the human brain responsible for language], doses of a potion that might turn them into fierce little reading machines, devourers of new syntax, fluent interpreters of the most lyrical complex grammar, so that the more difficult kind of sense writing might strive to make could find its appropriate Turing machine, and would be revealed to the reader with the delicacy the writer intended. . . . But these enhancements to Wernicke's areas in fact already exist, and they're called books."

As this wishful casting of spells may intimate, the books Marcus speaks of are not the kinds of books Franzen might champion: conventional social narratives promising pleasure sans difficulty. Ultimately Franzen's credo, as he expressed it nine years before Marcus threw down the gauntlet, is the need to attract and please readers. A declared enemy of "audience-friendly writing," Marcus is fearlessly on the side of difficulty: "entirely new syntactical byways," "a poetic aim that believes in the possibility of language to create ghostly frames of sense." Gertrude Stein, Samuel Beckett, and William Gaddis are among his older models, and these he opposes to a "narrative realist mode, which generally builds linearly on what has gone before, subscribes to cinematic verisimilitude, and, when it's not narrating, slaps mortar into an already stable fictional world." Accordingly, he bludgeons Franzen relentlessly: "Language is a poor medium for the kinds of mass entertainment that Franzen seems interested in." And: "He wants literary language to function as modestly as spoken language." And: "He seems desperately frustrated by writers who don't actively court their audiences, who do not strive for his specific kind of clarity, and who take a little too much pleasure in language."

So it is a fight rather than an argument, really — a fight over complexity versus ease, a fight that mostly mimics gang war, which is not so much a vigorous instance of manly bloodletting (though it is that too) as a dustup over prestige: who has the prior right to swagger in public. It cannot be an argument these two are having — meaning a debate between fundamentally differing positions — because both Franzen and Marcus are in stringent agreement. What they are in agreement about is the necessity of having a readership. Franzen's is large, Marcus's is decidedly smaller — a coterie perhaps, drawn to entirely new syntactical byways and similar hurdles. Each scorns the other's audience; each is content with his own. And both are preoccupied with the recitation of numbers — Franzen earnestly, with those best-seller millions, Marcus derisively, with something called "the Fog Index point spread." The Fog Index, he explains, provides statistical proof that Franzen's vocabulary beats Gaddis's by several school grades: Franzen's fog is even thicker than Gaddis's! Then there is the "Lexile Framework for Reading," according to which, Marcus points out, Gaddis's prose in *A Frolic of His Own* is "just slightly more readable than the Harry Potter series," while Franzen's far higher readability score is on a par with the abstrusely specialized vocabulary of a manual on how to lay brick. All this recondite mathematical taunting appears in an ample footnote designed to mock Franzen's commitment to popularity and his flaunted disdain for difficulty. Still, it is Gaddis, Marcus gloats, who, for all his simpler words and shorter sentences, remains the more complex writer. So: a punch in the eye for Franzen! The Cripps and the Bloods would feel right at home in this alley.

Out of the alley and along the culture's main concourse, both Franzen and Marcus have stumbled into the same deep public ditch — a nearly vacant trench in need of filler. Never mind that one believes in diversion and the other dreams of potions. If the two of them are equally touchy and contentious and competitive, what has made them so is the one great plaint they have in common: *the readers are going away.* Whether they are readers to be lured to Marcus's putative avant-garde experiments, or to Franzen's entertainments, it hardly matters. The readers are diminishing, they are going away.

Denis Donoghue, in an essay titled "The Defeat of Poetry," tells where they are going. An eminent literary scholar, and for thirty years a university professor, Donoghue is here speaking of American undergraduates: the newest crop of potential readers that novelists will try to harvest. "When I started teaching, at University College, Dublin many years ago," he reports,

> I urged students to believe that the merit of reading a great poem, play, or novel consisted in the pleasure of gaining access to deeply imagined lives other than their own. Over the years, that opinion, still cogent to me, seems to have lost much of its persuasive force. Students seem to be convinced that their own lives are the primary and sufficient incentive. They report that reading literature is mainly a burden. Those students who think of themselves as writers and take classes in "creative writing" to define themselves as poets or fiction writers evidently write more than they read, and regard reading as a gross expenditure of time and energy. They are not open to the idea that one learns to write by reading good writers.
>
> In class, many students are ready to talk, but they want to talk either about themselves or about large-scale public themes, independent of the books they are supposedly reading. They

are happy to denounce imperialism and colonialism rather than read "Heart of Darkness," *Kim,* and *A Passage to India* in which imperialism and colonialism are held up to complex judgment. They are voluble in giving you their opinions on race and its injustices, but they are tongue-tied when it is a question of submitting to the language of *The Sound and the Fury, Things Fall Apart,* and *A Bend in the River.* They find it arduous to engage with the styles of *Hard Times* and *The Wings of the Dove,* but easy to say what they think about industrialism, adultery, and greed.

So is that where the readers of the next generation are going: to the perdition of egotism and moralizing politicized self-righteousness? The case can be made — Franzen surmised this almost two decades ago — that these students will never evolve into discriminating readers; or, as Marcus would have it, their Wernicke's areas have been rendered infertile. Then where are they going, if not to Faulkner and Achebe and Naipaul? The answer is almost too hackneyed. To the movies; to television (hours and hours); to Googling obsessively (hours and hours), to tweeting and blogging and friending and texting (hours and hours); and undoubtedly also, when at the dentist's, to *People* magazine, where the celebrity photos outnumber the words. While concentrating on dispraising audience-friendliness, Marcus seems to have overlooked, or thinks it not worth mentioning (as Gertrude Stein, his predecessor in autonomous art, once put it): *there is no there there.* The audience, or most of it, has gone the way of the typewriter and the telephone booth and fedoras and stockings with seams.

Then what is to be done about the making, and the taking

in, of literature — specifically, in our time, the serious literary novel? Is Franzen right to blame popular electronic seductions for the novelist's problems? Is Marcus justified in rating the wizardry of language juxtaposition over the traditional novel's long heritage of "deeply imagined lives"? Is the realist novel, as he claims, merely a degraded device whereby "language is meant to flow, predigested, like liquid down a feeding tube"? (Does this, by the way, characterize any novel by Nabokov or Bellow?) As it turns out, Marcus does not altogether denigrate realism — he pauses to laud its "deep engineering" as a "brilliant feat" — but he faults it, in furious italics, because "*it has already been accomplished.*" According to this thesis, nothing is worth doing unless it has never been done before. But we have heard, and from a master, that ripeness — not newness — is all. Besides, why should one literary form lust to dispossess another? Why must there be a hierarchy, Experimentalism (pushing the envelope) on top, Realism (old hat) below? Mozart and jazz, for instance, live honorably together on the same planet. Marcus describes the style of writing he admires as "free of coherence, so much more interested in forging complex bursts of meaning that are expressive rather than figurative, enigmatic rather than earthly, evasive rather than embracing." He concludes: "I find it difficult to discover literary tradition so warmly embraced and coddled, as if artists existed merely to have flagrant intercourse with the past, guaranteed to draw a crowd, but also to cover that crowd in an old, heavy breading." Ah, now we are back at the old gang rumble. At Marcus's end of the alley, though, something smells stale, like old heavy breading. "Expressive rather than figurative," "enigmatic rather than earthly," "free of coherence," and all the rest: *it has already been accom-*

plished. The avant-garde's overused envelope was pushed long ago, and nothing is more exhaustedly old hat than the so-called experimental. Hoary superannuated abstract painting, consisting chiefly of colors and planes, practiced by Mondrian, born 1872; by Kandinsky, also born 1872; by Delaunay, born 1885. Experimental music, micro-macrocosmic rhythmic structure à la John Cage, born 1912. Experimental writing, as in Dadaism, a movement begun in 1916. And here comes Ben Marcus, self-styled enigmatic experimentalist innovator, born 1967.

All the foregoing may be mesmerizing for those in the book business who are drawn to the spectacle of writerly acrobatics — to the shifting highs and lows of publicity — but it is beside the point and misleading. Except for the few preeminent novelists who have earned, via stature and money, the power to stand aloof, serious fiction writers *are* pressed by elements external to the imagination's privacies, and external also to the secrets of language (including the clarinet that attends the semicolon). But in searching for the key to the Problem of the Contemporary Novel (or Novelist), there are cupboards where it is useless to look. And there are reasons that do not apply: writers vying for the highest rung of literary prestige; potential readers distracted by the multiplicity of storytelling machines. Feuds and jealousies are hardly pertinent, and the notorious decline of reading, while incontrovertible, may have less to do with the admittedly shaky situation of literary fiction than many believe.

The real trouble lies not in what is happening, but in what is not happening.

What is not happening is literary criticism.

But wait. Why should the novel care about that? Novels *will* be written, whatever the conditions that roil around them. The novel is an independent art, secretive in its gestation, a living organism subject to a hundred protean characterizations. Of all its touted representations, the most irritable is Henry James's "loose baggy monster," while the most insistently self-proclaiming is Flaubert's "*Madame Bovary, c'est moi.*" The scholar-critic Robert Alter, if less succinct, is more suggestive: "In the novel," he writes, "the possibility always exists, and is often exploited, to zigzag rapidly between different narrative stances, voices, styles, to improvise and jiggle with new options of narration, to flaunt the mechanisms of narration as they are deployed and invented." He goes on to cite "the elaborately decorous omniscient narrator of *Tom Jones* . . . the nested first-person narrations of *Wuthering Heights,* the purportedly impassive narratorial manipulator of *style indirect libre* in *Madame Bovary,* the shifting verbal vaudeville of *Ulysses.*" (A definition as capacious as this one should go far to reconcile the boys in the alley.)

The novel, then, in all its forms and freedoms, is not in danger; nor is the born novelist — dwindling audiences and the intrusions of pixels notwithstanding. The next Saul Bellow may at this moment be playing patty-cake in his crib — or we may have to wait another two hundred years or so for a writer equal in intellect and vivacity and breadth to turn up. It hardly matters. The "fate of the novel," that overmasticated, flavorless wad of old chewing gum, is not in question. Novels, however they may manifest themselves, will never be lacking. What is missing is a powerfully persuasive, and pervasive, intuition for how they are connected, what they portend in the aggregate, how they comprise and color an era. A novel, it goes without saying, is an idiosyncrasy: it stands alone, it intends originality — and if it is commandeered by genius, it will shout originality. Yet the novels that crop up in any given period are like the individual nerves that make up a distinct but variegated sensation, or act in chorus to catch a face or a tone. What is missing is an undercurrent, or call it, rather (because so much rests on it), an infrastructure, of serious criticism.

This does not mean reviews. A reviewer is not the same as a critic; a case can be made (I will try to make it) that a reviewer is, in effect, the *opposite* of a critic, in the way that an architect is different, not in degree but in kind, from a mason, or in the way that a string theorist is different, though both employ mathematics, from a bookkeeper. Neither masons nor bookkeepers are likely to feel disparaged by this observation. Reviewers may be stung. Reviews, after all, are the sustenance of publishing. Reviews are indispensable: a book that goes unreviewed is a dud to its publisher, and a grief to its author. Besides, reviews through their ubiquity simulate the skin of a genuine literary culture — rather like those plastic faux-alligator bags sold everywhere, which can almost pass for the real thing. In newspapers and magazines, both print and electronic, in book clubs and blogs, in television interviews and in radio format, reviews proliferate more freely than ever before. And they have the advantage of accelerating and multiplying through undreamed-of new venues open to nonprofessionals. The book clubs, for instance. Book club reviewers are characterized, by and large, by earnestness and eagerness, and by a sort of virtuous communal glow: they are "amateur" in its root meaning — they are lovers, lovers of books. Some, or perhaps many, may also be amateur in the sense of being unskilled; but they practice reviewing privately, in the secluded warmth of a living room, within a circle of

friends, hence innocently. That these clubs are too often caught
in a kind of Möbius spiral, or chicken-and-egg conundrum, is
an ongoing curiosity: because they choose to read mainly bestsellers (e.g., *The Hunger Games,* or *Fifty Shades of Grey,* or
whatever currently tops the list), they appear simultaneously to
create these bestsellers.

Less innocent is the rise of the nonprofessional reviewer on
Amazon — though "rise" suggests an ascent, whereas this com-
puterized exploitation, through commerce and cynicism, of
typically unlettered exhibitionists signals a new low in public responsibility. Unlike the valued book club reviewer, who
may be cozily challenged by companionable discourse, Amazon's "customer reviewer" goes uncontested and unedited:
the customer is always right. And the customer, the star of this
shoddy procedure, controls the number of stars that reward
or denigrate writers. Amazon's unspoken credo is that anyone, or everyone, is well suited to make literary judgments —
so that a reader of chick lit (the term defines the reader), perhaps misled by ad hype (the term defines book marketing),
will howl with impatience at any serious literary fiction she
may have blundered into. Here is "Peggy of Sacramento (*see
my other reviews*)" grudgingly granting one ill-intentioned star
to a demanding contemporary novel: "boring slowness, hard
going, characters not even a mother could love." Or Tim: "A
thoroughly depressing book. The home life was not a pleasant
atmosphere in which to raise children." Most customer reviewers, though clearly tough customers when it comes to awarding
stars, are not tough enough — or well-read enough — for tragic
realism or psychological complexity. Amazon encourages na-
ïve and unqualified readers who look for easy prose and uplift-

ing endings to expose their insipidities to a mass audience. It is true that one can, on occasion, find on Amazon a literate, lively, penetratingly intelligent response: an artful golden minnow in a fetid sea, where both praise and blame are leveled by tsunamis of incapacity.

(Academic theorists equipped with advanced degrees, who make up yet another species of limited reviewers, are worthy only of a parenthesis. Their confining ideologies, heavily politicized and rendered in a kind of multisyllabic pidgin, have for decades marinated literature in dogma. Of these inflated dons and doctors it is futile to speak, since unlike the hardier customer reviewers, they are destined to vanish like the fog they evoke.)

And what of the professional reviewers? They count as writers, certainly; but few writers of fiction can be found among them. It may be that novelists wish to stick to writing novels, uninterrupted; or that competitiveness toward other people's books engenders a sour reluctance to celebrate a rival; or simply that reviewing is a skill antithetical to the fictive talent; or, less simply, that the reviewer's more modest stitches will not satisfy the wider ambition of the tapestry weaver who hopes to cover a wall. For all these reasons, and possibly more, most novelists, especially as they mature, tend to eschew reviewing. A good thing, too. The literary judgments even of novelists of consequence can be capricious — Virginia Woolf dismissing James Joyce, for example, or, more recently, V. S. Naipaul dissing Henry James:

> The worst writer in the world actually [Naipaul told an interviewer in Britain's *Literary Review*]. He never went out into the world.... He never risked anything.... He never thought he

should mingle in the crowd and find out what they were there for, or how they behaved. He did it all from the top of a carriage or the top of a coach. A lot of his writing is like that. And he exalts his material because he thinks this subject matter he alighted on — the grandeur of Europe and the grandeur of new American money — is unbeatable.

For generations of readers of *The Golden Bowl* and *The Princess Casamassima,* that Jamesian subject *has* been unbeatable, and is as worldly as the range of an expansively inquisitive mind can be; so it is a relief to know that Sir Vidia is not an incessant reviewer of his lowly contemporaries. And a relief also to recognize that though reviewers are, in their fashion, writers, they are not often Nobel-winning novelists.

Frequently they are publishers. In fact, a book's publisher is its first and perhaps most influential reviewer. How a book is "positioned" — i.e., described to the sales staff and in catalogues and flap copy — can nearly seal its fate, or at least condition its reception. In the case of a literary novel (the term intends a dangerous elitism), in-house positioning can snuff it with a word. That word is "midlist"; whoever coined it merits hanging. It emits defeatism. It promises failure. An emblem of noblesse oblige, it reminds publishers that they still owe a modicum of responsibility to the higher literary culture. But what executive editor or vice president will want to back, with dollars and fanfare, a novel tainted by the whisper of midlist? Even so, the writer privileged to be included in this doubtful category is a thousand times more fortunate than the serious literary novelist who is not likely to be published at all. A publishing house is not an eleemosynary organization: who today would publish Proust? (An inapt question, since no mainstream press was willing to publish Proust *then:* initially he paid out of his own pocket to get his work into print; and nowadays, with digital self-publishing readily available, it's every writer his own Proust.) Besides, your typical publisher as first-stage reviewer is more prone to favor treacle — to treat an uplifting pedestrian fiction as a genuine literary novel — than to honor the real right thing. Or, on the other hand, to gussy up the real right thing with commerce-pleasing fakery: only imagine *Pride and Prejudice* hyped, in suitable shiny jacket, as a bodice ripper. Still, in crannies here and there (the golden minnow factor), and again in the larger houses, there remain editors possessed by the old calling — the bringing to light of darker worlds, heretical glimpses, adamantine art.

I stand accused, nevertheless, of misleading. Book club members, Amazon customers, postcolonialist English departments, canny publishing executives — are these what we mean when we speak of reviewers? Aren't the *real* reviewers the people who do it for a living, the talented hired hands who write regularly for a single periodical, or the diligent scattershot freelancers? In brief, that body of readers-by-occupation whose expertise, we feel, ought to make up, collectively, a society's cultural temperament. Were there space enough and time, it might be so — this notion of a powerful undercurrent of literary intelligences, streams crossing streams, all flowing out of one great governing critical headwater; but it is not so. The professional reviewer, given fifteen hundred words or less to consider a work of fiction, must jump in and jump out again: an introductory paragraph, sometimes thematic though often not, a smattering of plot, a lick at idea (if there is one), and then the verdict, the definitive cut —

yes or no. A sonnet, with worse constraints, or a haiku's even tinier confines, can conjure philosophies and worlds. A review, whose nature is prose, is not permitted such legerdemain. Nor is criticism. Yet what separates reviewing from criticism — pragmatically — are the reductive limits of space; the end is always near. What separates criticism from reviewing — intrinsically — is that the critic must summon what the reviewer cannot: horizonless freedoms, multiple histories, multiple libraries, multiple metaphysics and intuitions. Reviewers are not merely critics of lesser degree, on the farther end of a spectrum. Critics belong to a wholly distinct phylum.

This is a phylum that, at present, hardly exists. When, a few years ago, and in the mode of a social experiment, the *New York Times Book Review* asked a pool of writers to name the best novel of the past twenty-five years, the results were partly predictable and considerably muddled. Toni Morrison's *Beloved,* a tale of slavery and its aftermath, won the most votes. Philip Roth, John Updike, Don DeLillo, and Cormac McCarthy were substantially represented. In an essay musing on the outcome of an exercise seemingly more quixotic than significant, A. O. Scott, a *Times* reviewer, noted that the choices gave "a rich, if partial and unscientific picture of American literature, a kind of composite self-portrait as interesting perhaps for its blind spots and distortions as for its details." Or call it flotsam and jetsam. You could not tell, from the novels that floated to the top, and from those bubbling vigorously below, anything more than that they were all written in varieties of the American language. You could not tell what, taken all together, they intimated in the larger sense — the tone of their time. A quarter century encompasses a generation, and a generation does have a composite feel to it. But here nothing was composite, nothing joined these disparate writers to one another — only the catchall of the question itself, dipping like a fishing net into the sea of fiction and picking up what was closest to the surface, or had already prominently surfaced. All these novels had been abundantly reviewed — piecemeal. No reviewer had thought to set *Beloved* beside Philip Roth's *The Plot Against America* (both are political novels historically disguised) to catch the cross-reverberations. No reviewer had thought to investigate the possibly intermarried lineage of any of these works: what, for instance, has Nick in DeLillo's *Underworld* absorbed from the Nick of Fitzgerald's *The Great Gatsby*? The novels that rose up to meet the *Book Review*'s inquiry had never been suspected of being linked, whether horizontally or vertically. It was as if each one was a wolf-child reared beyond the commonality of a civilization; as if there was no recognizable thread of literary inheritance that could bind, say, Mark Helprin to Raymond Carver. Or if there was, no one cared to look for it. Nothing was indebted to nothing.

Many readers shrugged off this poll as entertaining trivia, or as run-of-the-mill editorial attention-seeking. Yet something culturally important came of it. It revealed, blazingly, what was missing, and has long been missing, in American letters: criticism that explains, both ancestrally and contemporaneously, not only how literature evolves, but how literature influences and alters the workings of human imagination. Here, to illustrate, is Harold Bloom, avatar and prescient forerunner, tracing — via Walt Whitman's *Song of Myself* — just such a pattern of cross-generational transfusion:

Like its major descendants — T. S. Eliot's *The Waste Land,* Hart Crane's *The Bridge,* Wallace Stevens's *Notes Toward a Supreme Fiction,* William Carlos Williams's *Paterson,* Conrad Aiken's *The Kid,* A. R. Ammons's *Sphere,* John Ashbery's *A Wave* — *Song of Myself* is an internalized quest-romance, whose antecedents include the long English Romantic tradition of falling in love with the poet's failure. That tradition goes from Wordsworth's *The Excursion* and Coleridge's nightmare *Rime of the Ancient Mariner* on through Shelley's *Alastor* and Keats's *Endymion* to Browning's ruined questers and the daemonic defeats of poets by their antithetical muse in Yeats.

This is Bloom's familiar messianism at work: the dazing fulfillment of a desired critical project before it has properly begun. And here also is James Wood, elucidating the design of that desire, not in one of his grand critical essays but merely in a short public letter making the case for Flaubert as the founder of the modern novel:

Our indebtedness, whether we like it or not, extends to, among other things: the fetishizing of visual detail; the inverted relationship between background and foreground detail (or habitual and dynamic detail); the sacralization of art; the privileging of the music of style over the recalcitrance of "unmusical" subject matter (Flaubert's famous desire to write a book about nothing); the agonizing over aesthetic labor — all this looks pretty new, and different in many ways from Balzac's great achievements and solutions, not least because these new Flaubertian anxieties cannot be solutions. You might say that Flaubert founds realism and simultaneously destroys it, by making it so aesthetic: fiction is real and artificial at once. And I could have added two other elements of modernity: the refinement of "free indirect style"; and the relative plotlessness of Flaubert's novels. All this is why different writers — realists, modernists and postmodernists — from Stephen Crane to Ian McEwan, from Kafka to Nabokov to Robbe-Grillet, all owe so much to Flaubert.

The key, then, is indebtedness. The key is connectedness. If Wood cannot read Flaubert without thinking of McEwan, neither can he read McEwan without thinking of Flaubert. In this single densely packed paragraph (though he is not usually so compact), Wood reflects on how scenes are constructed; how art imitates faith; how aesthetics can either combine with or annihilate what passes for the actual world. And also: the relation of story to the language that consumes it, and the descent of literature not only from one nation to another, but from one writer to another — all the while clinging to a unitary theme, the origin and nature of the modern. Such an imperial analysis has both a Darwinian and a biblical flavor: evolution mixed with Genesis.

Perhaps because Wood is partial to realism (though not to "magical" or — his term — "hysterical" realism), he is sometimes faulted for narrow sympathies, and for deprecating those styles and dispositions that escape the bounds of his particular credo. Yet a critic is nothing without an authoritative posture, or standard, or even prejudice, against which an opposing outlook or proposition can be tested. To keep to a point of view is itself a critical value. The grand historic example of critical authority is Samuel Johnson, whose unyielding mastery of a position was such that to affirm it wholly was never easy, while to dissent from it was still more difficult — but the assertion itself roused the mind. In just this sense of instigating counterbalance, Wood is a necessary contemporary goad.

For an extended period — an anomaly in a culture of kaleidoscopically rapid shifts — he stood alone, a promontory of notice and prestige. A stimulus and a goad, yes, but companionless. On the American scene, from the New England Transcendentalists to the Southern Agrarians to the New Critics to the New York Intellectuals, linkages and public movements have been more nearly the norm. At least part of the reason for isolated renown may be what has come to be called a "platform" — the critic's identification with a single journal. George Steiner's hierarchical elitism, for instance, once dominated the *New Yorker*, defining for its readers what criticism ought to do. Consistency of this order has its public benefit (steady access to a singular mind), but after a time an evolving disadvantage creeps in: the pace, the voice, the tone, the habits of phrasing, have grown too familiar. (And also the occasional verbal tic: older readers may recall Steiner's evocation of lofty models, such as "an Aristotle," "a Mozart," as if there might be several of each to choose from.) Where dazzlement is routinely expected, it ceases to dazzle. A critic is fresher when less territorial, a restless pilgrim bird with multiple nests.

And the contrapuntal — contrapuntal, that is, to Wood's prevailing clef — has begun to assert itself, as will happen when a notable critic commands an overriding baton. A case in point: as long ago as 1925, Edmund Wilson, in an essay on Henry James, took issue with Van Wyck Brooks, a leading critic of that burgeoning if quarrelsome era. Wilson's subject, it turned out, was not so much James as it was Brooks's influence on the critical idiom of the hour. Brooks had disparaged James as "an enchanted exile in a museum-world"—a fore-echo of Naipaul's "from the top of a carriage or the top of a coach" (that oddly redundant vehicular sneer). "The truth is," Wilson wrote, "Mr. Brooks cannot help expecting a really great writer to be a stimulating social prophet." And again: "It is precisely because Mr. Brooks's interest is all social and never moral that he has missed the point of James's art." In arguing that James eschewed overt societal indictment because he was "preoccupied simply with the predilection of moral character," Wilson was intending to unseat Brooks's position as arbiter of what a significant literature should properly pursue: Brooks, he insisted, was a "preacher." Certainly Wilson was pushing against a view that in the following decade would support the rise of the blunt and blatant proletarian novel. And whether or not it was Wilson's dissent, in combination with gathering mutations of taste, that finally deposed him, the fading of Brooks as a preeminent critic was such that today he is mainly forgotten. Not, however, that Brooks was deprived of an ironic victory. Wilson in all his expansiveness went on to become, among manifold other literary paths zealously trod, a conscious social critic. And as a multivalent pundit, he argued with Nabokov over the nuances of Russian translation, popularized the complex history of the Dead Sea Scrolls, and wrote reverberatingly about everything from burlesque shows to the stock market crash to what he termed "the special psychology of reviewers."

Wilson-versus-Brooks represents a purposeful clash of differing temperaments; but the contrapuntal critic can also turn up in the absence of deliberate opposition, out of the communal air, out of contrasting literary intuitions that begin now to be widely heard — and unlike Wilson, with no intent to diminish a lauded critic. The contrapuntals have, finally, appeared; they are here, and Wood is no longer lonely in his eminence. For Wood, the animating force, his engine of origins, is the crisis of belief and unbelief, of reality and sham: a metaphysical alertness. And something else, unspoken but speaking for itself: the conviction that criticism must be able to stand as literature in its own right.

The contrapuntals I have in mind (because they are visible everywhere, winging from nest to nest) are Adam Kirsch and Daniel Mendelsohn. Like Wood, each comes from — as in the ideologically minded exploratory phrase "Where are you coming from?" — a background of early, and deeply embedded, preoccupation. Mendelsohn is that uncommon contemporary presence, a master of the literature of ancient Greece. Kirsch is a poet, and more than that: he is in serious possession of the very thing that long ago alarmed John Blackwood, George Eliot's publisher, when, on first reading *Daniel Deronda,* he unhappily discovered "the Jewish element." (Kirsch is also in possession of what might be termed "the George Eliot element," the capacity to embrace intellectually, and inhabit sympathetically, discrete yet crucially intertwined cultures.) Both Kirsch and Mendelsohn follow Wilson in breadth, ranging at will beyond the immediately literary, Mendelsohn more peripatetically than Kirsch. Kirsch is closer to Wood in scrupulous attention to language, as one would expect of a poet, particularly one of formal inclination. Mendelsohn's paragraphs will freely employ relaxed popular speech, sometimes even tending toward the breezy, while at the same time tightly analytical.

Having fully assimilated the postmodernist leveling of high and low, he approaches film and television with the same brio as he might bring to a play by Euripides; or he will mingle the current with the classical, pointing out parallels (viz., "As Seinfeld and Aristotle both knew . . ."). Neither Mendelsohn nor Kirsch is as fierce a close reader as Wood, or drills into the work under inspection with the same fanatical eye. Kirsch has undertaken to penetrate the oceanic pages of the Talmud (albeit in English translation), *daf* by patient *daf*. He has published a biography of Disraeli and a comprehensive study of Lionel Trilling: impossible to conceive of Wood's being drawn to either figure. (Kirsch has, in fact, been described as Trilling's heir.) And Mendelsohn is the author of *The Lost*, a moving, exhaustive, and revelatory history of his family's Holocaust-devoured Polish branch that stands starkly apart from the critic's role.

In an analogy that is certainly inexact as to particulars, but nevertheless interestingly suggestive of how oddly and unexpectedly forked a life can be, Mendelsohn brings to mind the career of A. E. Housman, who as a ferociously contentious dry-as-dust Latin scholar was devoted, among others, to Manilius, a minor and mostly overlooked Roman poet and astrologer. All that side of Housman is half obliterated; what lasts are the lyrically bucolic verses that erupted from an unsuspected and yearningly tender inwardness. And for Mendelsohn, a disciplined early immersion in the rigor of the classics has somehow drawn out an appetite for the most tumultuous, even circus-like, aspects of the present scene: from Sophocles and Aristophanes, say, to *Mad Men* and *Downton Abbey*. Yet while this exuberant transmutation from one species of perception to another can never be predictable or stodgy, it can sometimes come at the cost of depth. The commanding if graver Kirsch, meanwhile, has moved with conceptual agility from the innate structural enclosures of the poem to elasticity, history, connectedness; and to steadfast literary authority fed by a sympathetic intellect. His ability to enter into the political, the societal, the moral — to leap from Reinhold Niebuhr to Harper Lee — distances his reach from the narrower channels of most contemporary critics.

Wellsprings are not always signposts; sometimes they are mazes. A classicist becomes a ringmaster of all the arts. A poet — a man of subtle letters — becomes a cultural interpreter.

But where, in all this, is Susan Sontag, who before her death at seventy-one was for more than forty years an inescapable omnipresence, named by the *New York Review of Books* as "one of the most influential critics of her generation"? She took the compliment as too easily obvious, and also obtuse; she preferred to think of herself as primarily a novelist: "I'm a storyteller," she proclaimed. Wood, skeptical of the historical novel as a form, lauded her final work of historical fiction, *In America,* as a successful exception. (His seemingly spirited endorsement, caught between a principle and its exemption, somehow ends feeling tacitly lukewarm.) Yet because Sontag was, incontrovertibly, that marmoreal edifice, a Public Intellectual, her self-recognition as such lofted her stature well above her plentiful essays, and surely beyond her four novels: it could not be said that she strove in the common critical stewpot. She knew herself to be royalty; she was no one's counterpart, and no one, she made plain, was her peer: she countenanced neither her like nor her unlike. She organized her own exile by ordering her burial in the venerable Père Lachaise cemetery in Paris, where Balzac, Proust, Colette, Gertrude Stein, and countless legendary luminaries are interred. And having lived as an American lioness of unsparing ambition, she willed herself to end as a foreigner in a foreign land: a literary, perhaps also a political, declaration. To formulate — to contribute to — a viable critical infrastructure, one must first be willing to be a part of it.

If Sontag — neither critical competitor nor critical confrere — made certain to steer clear of the hope for such an infrastructure, Leon Wieseltier has been its tutelary spirit and facilitator. As literary editor of the *New Republic* for more than three decades (until its transmigration into a digital afterlife), he presided over the magazine's matchless book section, inviting largeness and depth, imposing no constraints on space or theme. Himself a distinctive stylist and a revivifying cultural critic, he gave a moral shape to questions of aesthetics, and brought humanist perspectives to political thought. Under his influence, the critical essay flourished, whether touching on literature or philosophy or history or painting or music. It was under Wieseltier's eye that Kirsch started out, and it was Wieseltier who recruited Wood — then chief critic for the London *Guardian* — and introduced him to American readers.

As more and more review journals give up the ghost or, like the *New Republic,* turn cybernetically anti-literary, the shallower digital venues proliferate. There, where the long essay makes for uneasy reading, and reviews are mostly random and trivial and shrunk to fit the hither-and-yon notice of cafeteria-style readers, what chance is there for the notion of a serious and sustained critical surround? Yet large projects do not relate to chance, nor are they prone to be stymied by prevailing circumstances. Instead, they germinate out of necessity and will.

Begin with necessity. What is essential is a critical mass of critics pursuing the kind of criticism that can define, or prompt, or inspire, or at least intuit, what is happening in a culture in a given time frame. What is needed are critics who can tease out hidden imperatives and assumptions held in common, and who will create the fertilizing conditions that underlie and stimulate a living literary consciousness. In this there is something almost ceremonial, or ceremoniously slow: unhurried thinking, the ripened long (or sidewise) view, the gradualism of deliberate shading. And here the critic comes closest to the historian by preparing the historian's path. When we speak of an era, an age, a period, a "climate of opinion" (as, in relatively recent times, the Georgian, the Edwardian, the Twenties, the Thirties, and so on), what is meant is a distillation of the insights, arguments, intimations, and even ideas of taste that the critics, in unintended concert, have amassed.

As for will — that conjoined sibling of necessity — much depends on the individual critic's perception of his task and its motives. In an essay reflecting on his own credo, Kirsch writes: "The critic participates in the world of literature not as a lawgiver or a team captain for this or that school of writing, but as a writer, a colleague of the poet and the novelist. Novelists interpret experience through the medium of plot and character, poets through the medium of rhythm and metaphor, and critics through the medium of other texts. This," he adds, "is my definition of 'serious criticism,' and I think it's essentially the same today as it was fifty years ago: a serious critic is one who says something true about life and the world." For Kirsch, lambent poet and discerning modulator, it is hardly a misstep to allow literary criticism to stand as an equal beside the novel and the poem, those deeply susceptible manifestations of the free imagination—since, after all, criticism too can be the source of the visual, the tactile, the emotive; but as a principle it may turn perilous. When the critic ventures too near the mode of the novel, aspiring to fathom the psyche of the author under review, or when he verges still more dangerously on the poet's power of metaphor, criticism then becomes akin to usurpation: to soulsnatching. Serious criticism is surely a form of literature, but the critic is not an artist with the artist's freedom of play. A critic is, at bottom, a judge, and judgment ought not to be tentative, or it is flat and useless. Neither ought it to be definitive in the way of drawing out a rounded, completed character that does not exist. And metaphor, when applied as personification, can be either revelation—or lie.

So, in asking for a broad infrastructure of critics and criticism to support and confirm a maturing literary organism, there will be caveats and skepticism. Still, should such an authentically engaged infrastructure ever come into being—or, rather, return, since (at least in our backward-looking trustfulness) it once prospered in large enough numbers to make a recognizable literary force—what would change? Professional reviewers, those hemmed-in heralds of the new, would trudge on as before, useful as always. Prudent publishers would go about their business of expediently touting the sentimental or the shocking while marginally tolerating the serious. Readers would continue to drift away, seduced and socialized by the ever-breeding pixels. The boys in the alley—sophisticated armies on a darkling plain—would continue to clash over accessibility and iconoclasm. But for unfulfilled readers and writers who fret over the neglect of the literary novel, something instinctually different might begin to hover: a hint of innate kinship, a backdrop, the white noise of the era that claims us all. In times that are made conscious of the air they breathe — a consciousness that only a critical infrastructure can supply — the varieties of literary experience become less antagonistic than inquisitively receptive. In the age we have learned to call Victorian, Disraeli and Oscar Wilde, novelists (and spirits) as unlike as can be imagined, evince a certain virtuoso interplay: we know this because criticism has taught us how to see it.

When Lionel Trilling reigned at Columbia, Edmund Wilson, Irving Howe, and Alfred Kazin enlivened the magazines, decade upon decade. Today there are inklings of who might constitute a potential critical aggregate, beginning with the legacy of John Updike, pressing on with essay after essay for forty years: self-evidently, the prophetic Harold Bloom, the scholar-poet Geoffrey Hartman, the formidably rounded and witty Joseph Epstein, the exquisitely indispensable Helen Vendler, the philosopher of literature Bernard Harrison; also Dana Gioia, Edward Mendelson, Richard Howard, Robert Alter, Morris Dickstein, Joyce Carol Oates, Laura Miller, Edward Alexander, Sven Birkerts, Martin Rubin, Michael Dirda, Linda Hall, Christopher Beha, William Giraldi, William Deriesewicz, Thomas Mallon, Wyatt Mason, Ruth Franklin, Louis Menand, Jed Perl, Phillip Lopate, Camille Paglia, Michael Gorra, Arthur Krystal — a range of status, age, consistency of publication, breadth of attentiveness, depth of desire, level of pugnacity. These, and others I have failed to mention, some perhaps in embryo, a few busy elsewhere as poets or novelists — not even these are enough. Passions and principles are copious beyond the anxieties of Franzen and Marcus, whose chief urgencies appear to be who will read. The better question is not who will read, or how they will read, but *why*.

And why really? To catch hold of the tincture and pitch of the hour, the why of the moment, the why of what led to the moment, the why of what may come of the moment, the frights and the fads, the hue and the cry, the why of what is honorable and what is not, the why of what is true and what is lie. It is the *why* that implicates and judges readers, and reviewers, and publishers, and bestseller lists; and novelists. *No novel is an island, entire of itself.* And it is again the *why* that tells us how superior criticism — the novel's ghostly twin — not only unifies and interprets a literary culture, but has the power to imagine it into being.

Figures

THE MOST ELEVATED BOOK CLUB IN THE HIS-
tory of American literary commerce had forty thousand subscribers but only three members, and was organized mainly
to make money. It was endorsed by a poet of renown: "Poets
and Professors and all those whose love of books exceeds
their love of automobiles," he wrote, "will welcome a chance
to save in excess of 50% on their book purchases." The club,
of course, was a marketing venture, and its entrepreneurial
sales force consisted of Lionel Trilling, Jacques Barzun, and
W. H. Auden (it was he who trumpeted the discount). Initiated in 1951 and named The Readers' Subscription, it mim-
icked the very successful Book-of-the-Month Club, with this
difference: it was consistently and confidently highbrow.
Barzun and Trilling, professorial colleagues at Columbia University, had, in fact, together invented the term "culture" as
we now know it — or so Barzun claimed in a 2011 review of
Adam Kirsch's *Why Trilling Matters,* a robust attempt to reas-
sess and resurrect Trilling's currently faded stature.

But by the time The Readers' Subscription was under way,

all three luminaries were already at the peak of their eminence, Barzun as a leading cultural historian, Trilling as the nation's most esteemed literary essayist, Auden as one of the two preeminent midcentury poets (the other being the towering Eliot). Each, then, was what Trilling was pleased to call a "figure": a distinctive thinker or artist who in one way or another stands for the inmost meaning of an era; an interpreter of society and its mainspring. Their common task as facilitators and admen was to select the books offered to subscribers, and to accompany each choice with a clarifying and enriching critical essay. The themes were various, but no volume was less than serious. Auden, for instance, wrote on Colette, Dostoyevsky, Robert Graves, Philip Larkin, John Betjeman, Eliot, Stravinsky, Berlioz, Faulkner, Muriel Spark, Tolkien, Hannah Arendt, and more. Surprisingly, Trilling took up subjects like audio recordings, contemporary theater ("It is not true that I hate the theater"), movies (chiefly Ingmar Bergman), nudity, architecture, James Baldwin, Golding's *Lord of the Flies,* Lawrence Durrell, James Agee, *The Wind in the Willows* ("not one of the sacred books of my childhood, but it might have been"), Isak Dinesen, Bellow's *The Adventures of Augie March* ("in the comic tradition"), and other ruminations one might not have expected. Barzun, meanwhile, was reflecting on Montaigne ("It was a hill, really, that Montaigne lived on and drew his name from"), Dürer, Virginia Woolf's diaries, Henry James's autobiography, Oscar Wilde, Japan, Eskimos, the origin of language, Proust, D. H. Lawrence, Shaw, Molière, and, in Barzun's own phrase, an encompassing "sense of history."

There was a kind of playful daring in the vastness of these

choices, and Barzun, describing the companionable meetings that led to the final decisions, revealed that they were
sometimes lightened by the mutual composition of cleri-
hews. He quoted one of his own: "Henry James / did not
name names, / but all the Bostonians knew / who was who."
None of this could disguise the gravity that enveloped not
only the advantageous undertakings of the "club," but the
literary tone of the period itself. In an ambitious novel Trilling
left unfinished, a character declaims his belief in what was
then all-important: "novel or nothing." But it was also a time
of high art or nothing, an Arnoldian idea soon to be scattered and dissolved by the coming of the Beats — for whom
"the best which has been thought and said" was turned, ec-
statically, into "the best which / have thought and said." The
figure, with all its restrained and dignified sobriety, was being ousted by bards with beards and zithers and weed. And
today, half a century later, the figure is no more. Even the
pinnacle of fame cannot make a figure: who can conceive of
Philip Roth, or Saul Bellow, as an equivalent of Trilling?

Yet we *can* think of them as critics, at least as a sideline —
though Roth's *Reading Myself and Others,* together with
his *Shop Talk: A Writer and His Colleagues and Their Work,*
could, all on their own, qualify anyone less anointed to be
seen as a significantly ample critic. And Bellow poured out
essay after essay, catching in his critical net everything from
Mozart to Jerusalem to preliterate societies to Wyndham
Lewis to Khrushchev, all via a muscular intellect unafraid to
be provocative and against the grain. He practiced criticism
much as Augie might, "go[ing] at things as I have taught
myself, free-style." In the course of his 1970 Nobel lecture he

asked, "And art and literature, what of them? Well," he answered, "there is a violent uproar, but we are not absolutely dominated by it. We are still able to think, to discriminate, and to feel. The purer, subtler, higher activities have not succumbed to fury or to nonsense. Not yet. Books continue to be written and read. It may be more difficult to cut through the mind of the modern reader, but it is still possible to reach the quiet zone." It was a hopeful but disenchanted talk.

Nearly fifty years on, there is very little left of the quiet zone, and the fury and the nonsense may have increased, thanks to the proliferation of communication devices not dreamed of when Bellow accepted his medal. He was of the generation of the founders of The Readers' Subscription, but too restless to have been counted among them as a likely fourth: who can imagine him sitting diligently in meetings while now and then spouting a clerihew or two?

Bernard Malamud, born a year before Bellow, was also a contemporary of the club triumvirate. Himself a figure, one of unique idiom and feelingful moral sensibility, his narrative irony never devolved into raw cynicism. This set him apart from the newer cohort of insouciant novelists who came into prominence decades after The Readers' Subscription was long forgotten and at least two of its members obscured by time and change; and perhaps it is easier now to see him among them, patiently abstracted in a corner of the sofa, encircled by angels from Harlem and impoverished grocers, shoemakers, and rabbinical students, all invisibly gyrating overhead.

Novel or Nothing: Lionel Trilling

One of the several advantages of living long is the chance to witness the trajectory of other lives, especially literary lives; to observe the whole, as a biographer might; or even, now and then, to reflect on fame with the dispassion of the biblical Koheleth, for whom all eminences are finally diminished. When we look around at the contemporary scene, we are in the dark, we cannot tell who will live on into the next generation, and who will be dismissed or, worse yet, eclipsed and forgotten. The luminaries of our youth and our prime may turn out to be strangers in the world of our old age.

The "we" and the "our" of the previous sentences are readily seen to be usurpations of Lionel Trilling's characteristic manner—or would be, if Trilling's prose style, and Trilling himself, were familiar to twenty-first-century readers. But Trilling's stature, once prodigious, is so reduced as to have become a joke to certain young critics who favor flippancy and lightness and who, if they are aware of Trilling at all, have learned to despise what he called "moral realism." Unlike Eliot's self-anointed "I," intended as the voice of a visiting archbishop, if not a materializing archangel, Trilling's all-embracing "we" had the effect both of companionable intimacy and of shared authority. It also implied a kind of humanist common sense, what every honest intellect will acknowledge in contemplating the exigencies of mortal existence. "We" carried certainty and conviction, and an openness to the serious and the tragic that Trilling in his later work would identify as sincerity and authenticity.

The breadth of Trilling's renown can hardly be understood today. He was a professor of literature at a major university who was at the same time a "figure" (a term he honored) in the culture at large. And what was he really? An essayist; and it is tempting to say, given the expository clamor of the moment—its short views and skimpy topicality—*merely* an essayist. Yet no present-day magazine writer or blogger or reviewer or critic can aspire to what Trilling as essayist encompassed: his aim was nothing less than to define, and refine, civilization. He meant not only to comment or discriminate or analyze or judge, but to "stand for something." And at his death at age seventy in 1975, what he finally stood for was a scrupulously perceptive and sinuously shaded interpretation of the moral life as expressed in the literature of the West. If the idea of *sage* could be applied to any American essayist after Emerson, that is what he had become. A more modulated perspective would settle for Trilling as the most discerning, the most reasoned, and certainly the most celebrated critic of his time.

Sage? Essayist? Critic? He did not wish it. It was neither his desire nor his plan. The acclaim that came to him, at forty-three, with the publication of *The Liberal Imagination*—a collection of ruminations affirming, as he put it, "the inevitable intimate, if not always obvious, connection between literature and politics" in the light of the mind's "great primal act of imagination"—

was gratifying, but it could not satisfy his earliest and most urgent intent. In a public lecture in 1971 (he was then sixty-six years old) he permitted himself an astonishing confession — astonishing, it was later revealed, only to his disbelieving audience. "I am always surprised," he said, "when I hear myself referred to as a critic ... If I ask myself why this is so, the answer would seem to be that in some sense I did not ever undertake to be a critic. The plan that did please my thought was certainly literary, but what it envisaged was the career of a novelist. To this intention, criticism, when eventually I began to practice it, was always secondary, an afterthought: in short, not a vocation but an avocation."

Yet this overt admission of self-repudiation had frequently been enacted privately. Portions of Trilling's notebooks, published after his death, disclosed remorseful longing, hidden competitiveness, envious ambition. He envied Hemingway, whose vitality in his "most foolish postures" Trilling saw as a model and a reproach. He envied Jack Kerouac, "not wanting K's book to be good." He envied instinct, physicality, manliness. He scorned his university colleagues as effete. "My being a professor and a much respected and even admired one is a great hoax," he wrote bitterly. "Suppose I were to dare to believe that one could be a professor and a man! and a writer!" The writer, he insisted — he meant the writer as novelist — was a man of action, carrying "his death warrant in his pocket."

It was more than simple yearning. He had the will for it — the compulsion, even under the conditions of his professorial constraints, even while engaged in the opposing rhetoric and argumentum of the essays, to commit to a novel. *The Middle of the Journey* — believed to be Trilling's sole long fiction — was published the year before *The Liberal Imagination,* with a very different reception for each: heated praise for the essays, coolness toward the fiction. The disparities of execution were considerable. The complex prose of the essays gave way, in the novel, to plainness—passages of spare, often sparse, narrative logically plotted, and clear colloquial dialogue. The tone was objective and straightforward and nearly bare of imagery, though not of descriptive force or drama. The drama was in the theme, and the theme carried a death warrant in its pocket: the baleful predicament of a brilliant though wayward American, a former secret agent for the Soviets who abandons the Party and is consequently in danger of his life. In an important—and vehement—introduction to a reissue of the novel almost thirty years after its initial publication, Trilling confirmed what had anyhow been generally surmised: that the character of his Communist defector, Gifford Maxim, had been inspired by Whittaker Chambers, with whom Trilling had been acquainted as an undergraduate at Columbia. It was not long before reality intervened to shift speculation into certainty:

> From my first conception of it, my story was committed to history—it was to draw out some of the moral and intellectual implications of the powerful attractions to Communism felt by a considerable part of the American intellectual class during the Thirties and Forties. But although its historical nature and purpose are attested to by the explicit reference it makes to certain of the most momentous events of our epoch, the book I wrote in 1946–1947 and published in 1947 did not depict anyone who was a historical figure. When I have said this, however, I must go on to say that among the characters of my story there is one

who had been more consciously derived from actuality than any of the others. . . . This person was Whittaker Chambers.

But only a few months after my novel was published, Chambers' status in history underwent a drastic change. The Hiss case broke upon the world and Chambers became beyond any doubt a historical figure.

The notoriously controversial espionage trial of Alger Hiss turned on Chambers's testimony from his knowledge of the Communist underground. The issue was treason, and Hiss, a disarming and plausibly earnest former State Department official who had once been a protégé of Justice Felix Frankfurter, was convicted of perjury, while Chambers was everywhere roundly vilified as a disreputable conspirator and liar favored by Nixon and the redbaiting Senator McCarthy. But what concerned Trilling, both in the unfolding of his novel and in the bitter polemics of his later reflections on it, was the obstinate reluctance of virtue-minded progressives to accept the facts of Stalinist perfidy. "At this distance in time," he wrote in 1975, "the mentality of the Communist-oriented intelligentsia of the Thirties and Forties must strain the comprehension even of those who, having observed it at first hand, now look back upon it, let alone of those who learn about it from such historical accounts of it as have been written. That mentality was presided over by an impassioned longing to believe. . . . Once the commitment to belief had been made, no evidence might, or could, bring it into doubt. Whoever ventured to offer such evidence stood self-condemned as deficient in good will." These few sentences, written in hindsight, still carry the fury of Trilling's aim in *The Middle of the Journey:* to expose what he deemed the hollowness of those middle-class fellow travelers — "radical intellectuals, and those who did not claim that epithet but modestly spoke of themselves as liberal or progressive or even only democratic" — who denied "the reality which lay behind the luminous words of the great promise."

In Trilling's scheme of moral accountability they are Arthur and Nancy Croom, a goodhearted, do-gooding young couple summering in the country. The Crooms invite their friend John Laskell, who has nearly died from a devastating illness, to recuperate in their pastoral village. Gifford Maxim arrives to join the little group, though he is unwelcome: the Crooms despise and condemn him as a doctrinal deserter. An ideological conflict erupts over the death, through her father's drunken blow, of a fragile neighborhood child. The liberal Crooms have always sympathized with Duck, the ne'er-do-well father, frequently hiring him for odd jobs on their property. Unreliable as he may be as a man, he is nevertheless a poor and ill-spoken laborer, a victim of his class in an indifferent society; it is the flaws of society that have made him what he is. As Arthur frames it, "social causes, environment, education or lack of education, economic pressure, the character-pattern imposed by society, in this case a disorganized society, all go to explain and account for any given individual's action." Then Nancy: "It's not his fault," she cries out in Duck's defense, appalled by his careless brutality to the child yet unwilling, like Arthur, to assign guilt or blame; unwilling also to let the man return to the work he needs. "But I couldn't stand him around me. I'd think of it all the time. I couldn't stand seeing him. And yet it's not his fault, it's not." To which Maxim, the repentant Communist who has repudiated social determinism, replies, "In my system there is one thing your system lacks. In my system, although there is never-ending responsibility, there is such a thing as mercy." He goes on:

> Duck can be forgiven. I can forgive him because I believe that God can forgive him. You see, I think his will is a bad one, but not much more, not different in kind from other wills. And so you and I are opposed. For you — no responsibility for the individual, but no forgiveness. For me — ultimately absolute responsibility for the individual, but mercy. Absolute responsibility: it is the only way that men can keep their values, can be thought of as other than mere *things*. These matters that Arthur speaks of — social causes, environment, education — do you think they really make a difference between one human soul and another? In the eyes of God are such differences of any meaning at all?

The Crooms are horrified — has Maxim turned insane? This is religious talk; it veers into crazy mysticism. Laskell, renewed and illuminated, finds a middle path between Maxim's fevered metaphysics and the Crooms' empty detachment from individual culpability. And when he parts from the Crooms, it is in relief and disillusionment: their friendship is at an end.

The Middle of the Journey is a very good novel, far superior to how it has long been rated. As a political novel, it has not grown stale; the politics of belief are with us still. As a novel of ideas, and of elastic characterization and freely flowing incident, it keeps clear of positions held by pasteboard symbols masking as persons. Laskell's engagement with Duck's little daughter is deft and intimate, throwing off glints of teasing charm. Eros makes its unexpected appearance on a riverbank. Gestures and conversations ring true. And overall, the tone is level and so-

ber, reflecting an invalid's fatigued notice as Laskell reawakens
to sharper seeing — observation becoming revelation. A good
novel, then; even a very good novel; but subjected to scorn by
Trilling's contemporaries, and not yet escaped from their judgment. "The attack on my novel," he recorded — it was a lasting resentment — "that it is gray, bloodless, intellectual, without
passion, is always made with great personal feeling, with anger. — How dared I presume?"

As Trilling saw it, what was being questioned was his right
to be a novelist at all. His determination to become one was regarded as impermissible literary transvestism. He had made his
reputation as an essayist, a thinker, an inquirer into the nature
of culture. Lawrence, Conrad, Mann, Kafka, Orwell, and Mat-
thew Arnold were among his touchstones. His groundbreaking
studies of novelists took in (in *The Liberal Imagination* alone)
Henry James, Sherwood Anderson, Mark Twain, Theodore
Dreiser, Rudyard Kipling, and F. Scott Fitzgerald; a longer work
was given over solely to E. M. Forster. In an essay of provocative
psychological audacity, he dared to say of Jane Austen, "She is
the first to be aware of the Terror which rules our moral situation. . . . She herself is an agent of Terror."

All these unflinching critical sentiments were distinguished
by a recognition of the link between feeling and what Trilling
construed as "reality," whose always perilous shadow was illusion. "It can be said," he wrote, "that all prose fiction is a varia-
tion on *Don Quixote*. Cervantes sets for the novel the problem of
appearance and reality: the shifting and conflict of social classes
becomes the field of the problem of knowledge, of how we know
and how reliable our knowledge is." Elsewhere he defined fiction as carrying "the cultural assumptions that make politics,"

and he was willing to subsume gossip under politics, and vice versa. In brief: more than anyone in his generation, Trilling had penetrated into the secret workings of The Novel: he knew it, he understood it, as an evolving, breathing, expanding, connecting social organism. Then surely it behooved him to bring forth not merely a good novel, and not merely a very good novel, but a great novel? This he had not done. QED: since with all this capacity for greatness he had not produced a great novel, it must follow that he had produced a bad novel — gray, bloodless, intellectual, without passion. For the lauded critic who stakes his truth on a transcendent standard, there may be a lesson in it: do not try to practice what you preach, or your admirers will gather round to pick your bones.

The Middle of the Journey, despite its variegated successes, was in fact not nearly a great novel. Nor could it have been, and for a reason that cannot be laid at Trilling's feet: he wrote too soon. In 1947 the smell of executions in the cellar of Moscow's Lubyanka prison, headquarters of the KGB, had not yet risen to the nostrils of the world. He was compelled to write abstractly of evils that were revealed viscerally only much later. If the fearful idea of a death warrant inflamed the novelist's intent, it went beyond any threat to the American life of Gifford Maxim. Trilling could readily vivify those progressive intellectuals who spurned the reality behind "the luminous words of the great promise" — they were in his immediate circle. Of the brutish reality itself he could speak, in or out of fiction, only in the screening language of news items, of "politics": purges, show trials, espionage, the Hitler-Stalin pact. What came to be called the Great Terror would have to wait for its definitive exposure by a novelist who had endured it. Not until the publication in the West, in

1968, of Aleksandr Solzhenitsyn's *The First Circle,* and of *The Gulag Archipelago* in 1973, was the human suffering inflicted by the Gulag finally and universally assimilated by its doubters and skeptics.

But even before then—for those who, like Trilling, had eyes to see—it was possible to comprehend the lineaments of that suffering, in particular through the reports and testimonies of Koestler, Souvarine, Silone, Akhmatova, Orwell, Pasternak, and many others. From writers such as these, Trilling could deduce the primal ruthlessness of the Soviet system: he could deduce it, he could infer it, but he could not disinter it—not in the darker corridors of the fictive imagination (as in *House of Meetings* Martin Amis would, sixty years on, when the brokenness and the heinousness had long been laid incontrovertibly and bloodily bare). Inference is distanced cognition, not a cudgel, and Trilling's theme in *The Middle of the Journey* was nothing if it was not the reality of the cudgel. The mind that had uncovered terror in so seemingly pacific a source as *Mansfield Park* was prevented by simple chronology from closer, more fleshly knowledge of the conditions of the Gulag.

Still, it is reasonable to ask, if Trilling *had* known, with the completeness of a later time, the violently corporeal conditions of the Gulag, could he have *done* them—done them, that is, novelistically? Would he have had the blood, the passion, the death warrant in his pocket?

This is not a question that will ever be answered. He did not again approach, in fiction, a subject that intimated physical cruelty on a large scale, invoking the anguish of whole populations. To those who disparaged his novel, and to the few who regretted its failure, the letdown for Trilling appeared to be so complete that it must clearly choke off any future attempt at a sustained fiction. His was the cautionary tale of the critic who had published a handful of short stories and a single novel, which, justifiably, had no successor. As a literary thinker he was preeminent. As a novelist he was beaten.

But he was not beaten. "How dared I presume?" was not, as it turned out, the cry of defeat it looked to be; it was the herald of renewed ambition. Another novel — a second one — was under way, though it may have begun earlier, as a first novel. In any event, Trilling was wholeheartedly preoccupied with it in the years following the unhappy reception of *The Middle of the Journey.* Disappointment spurred him: in a letter to Richard Chase, a Columbia colleague, he confided that he hoped for a "richer, less shaped, less intellectual, more open" work. "I think the next one will be better," he said. Chastened yet emboldened, he confessed to his journal, "There comes an impulse to take myself more seriously, for although measured against what I admire I give myself no satisfaction, yet against what I live with I have something to say and give and might really interest myself — and all this gives to the novel a new validity — the notion is right and I begin to see it substantively."

Six decades were to pass before we were permitted to learn of this novel's existence. Untitled, it was left unfinished — cast out midway, after twenty-four chapters and a hundred and fifty pages. News of it has erupted like a secret exploding; yet all along it was hiding in plain sight in Columbia's Trilling archive. Columbia University Press has now brought it out as *The Journey Abandoned,* with a valuable introduction by Geraldine Murphy, the Trilling scholar who uncovered it, and who serves as its impeccable editor. And though Trilling had vowed a departure from the "intellectual," the new work was inevitably more so, since a number of its characters derived from the fevered arena of literary high culture. At the same time, and contrary to his hopes, Trilling's second venture was more enclosed than the first, where politics had led outward to intimations of the great world and its deadly upheavals. But the progress of Victor Hammell, the ambitious young biographer who is its hero, takes him largely into intricately internalized psychological musings. Professor Murphy's edition includes a preface by Trilling, or what she has chosen to present as a preface. To forestall easy mockery ("Henry James had the forbearance to *finish* a novel before writing its preface," for instance), one ought to consider Trilling's two opening sentences: "I am sure there is no need for me to explain why I do not want to make a precise formulation of my novel so early in the game. A novel must eventually be conceived through its writing even more than through its originating idea and an abstract statement of the story's impulses at this point might well freeze them and make them useless." Like any preface, this has a public voice—but it may also be the kind of explanatory statement that accompanies an inquiry to a publisher. Whether the manuscript ever fell under a publisher's eye apparently remains unknown. Nevertheless, to attach the term "preface," with its Jamesian reminders, to Trilling's searching reflections and suppositions is exactly right. It is James who presides over Trilling's aspiration; it is James whom he consciously summons, and who serves as his cicerone and mentor. During the period when Trilling was seriously at work on the novel, he was also writing an introduction to *The Princess Casamassima,* and it was here that he set down what must be regarded as his novel's true preface:

The Princess Casamassima belongs to a great line of novels which runs through the nineteenth century as, one might say, the very backbone of its fiction. These novels, which are defined as a group by the character and circumstance of their heroes, include Stendahl's *The Red and the Black,* Balzac's *Père Goriot* and *Lost Illusions,* Dickens' *Great Expectations,* Flaubert's *Sentimental Education;* only a very slight extension of the definition is needed to allow the inclusion of Tolstoy's *War and Peace* and Dostoyevsky's *The Idiot.*

The defining hero may be known as the Young Man from the Provinces. He need not come from the provinces in literal fact, his social class may constitute his province. But a provincial birth and rearing suggest the simplicity and the high hopes he begins with — he starts with a great demand upon life and a great wonder about its complexity and promise. He may be of good family but he must be poor. He is intelligent, or at least aware, but not at all shrewd in worldly matters. He must have acquired a certain amount of education, should have learned something about life from books, although not the truth.

This, fully elaborated, was Trilling's new theme, and also its line of literary descent. The idea appears again in the unfinished work's preface (the characterization we are obliged to use). "Think of him," he says of Vincent Hammell,

as practical, energetic, not a dreamer or a mooncalf. He has real talent and he does not have the mechanical "shyness" of a sensitive young hero; indeed, one of the notable things about him is his active charm. He has what in a young man passes for maturity. He is decent, generous; but he is achingly ambitious. He has considerable insight into the conditions of his society, he wishes to be genuine, a man of integrity; yet he also wishes to be successful. His problem is to advance his fortunes and still be an honest man. He is conscious of all the dangers; he is literate and knows the fates of Julian Sorel, of Rastignac, of Frederic Moreau — all the defeated and disintegrated young men of the 19th century cycle of failure. He, for his part, is determined not to make their mistakes.

How much Trilling knows! He has already warned himself not to risk knowing too much, lest his story "freeze." But his tone here is strangely after-the-fact — that of a critic who is discussing a recognizable character in an established novel he has frequently read with profit and appreciation. How can Vincent Hammell breathe and freely act if he is designed according to an acknowledged template, if he is swaddled in layers of social and psychological and literary preconceptions? A novelist must understand that one cannot imagine one's characters — they must be at liberty to imagine themselves. And this too Trilling understood: understood so well that he took care to instruct his characters in how to observe and judge independently, thereby imprisoning them ever more deeply in his own mind.

Vincent Hammell is a character prescribed. Born in a small town in the Midwest, he is the son of an optometrist. The time is the 1930s; money is scarce. The world of opportunity and hope lies, and lures, elsewhere, and the means of attaining it is through the life of letters. Vincent is a literary aspirant who has already abandoned a work on "nothing less grandiose than a history of American literature in the latter part of the nineteenth century" (Trilling's own field of scholarship, Professor Murphy notes). "I'm twenty-three," he tells his mother despairingly, "and my fine success consists of a quarter-time job at the university, a couple of days a month for the *Advertiser*, oh yes, and the pleasure of instructing ladies . . . in creative writing. Quite a success."

His release from these petty circumscriptions comes through an unexpected proposal from Harold Outram, the powerful director of the Peck Foundation. From a beginning as obscure as Vincent's, Outram contrived to gain importance and acclaim in successive stages: first as a critic, then as a novelist esteemed as "one of the legends of the new American promise," then as a radical agitator, then as an apostate from radicalism (a whiff of Whittaker Chambers again), then as the dean of a celebrated magazine (Chambers wrote for *Time*); and finally as the head of an influential cultural institution, the apogee of it all. But Vincent is cautioned against Outram by his former teacher, Teddy Kramer, a man "of such scrupulous intellectual honesty that he could bring no work to a satisfactory conclusion"—a trait Vincent equates with Kramer's "Jewish pride." "Let me tell you, Vincent," Kramer warns, "you will see [in Outram] a man utterly corrupt." According to Kramer, Outram is a danger and a sellout: he has abandoned literature's sacred calling for worldly domination.

Outram's offer to Vincent is dumbfounding—the chance to write the biography of the still living but elderly Jorris Buxton, the paramount figure of the age. Buxton's background borders on the improbable: a professor of Greek, a poet, a painter, a novelist—all this before his fortieth year, following which, Outram explains, "he became a physicist. He engaged a tutor and in a year he had learned everything that a brilliant student learns in

four years . . . everything he had learned seemed to be there inside him ready to be unfolded. That is, he was a genius. He went
to M.I.T. and his doctoral thesis is still famous. . . . He took jobs
in several of the great physical laboratories. He went to Europe
and studied mathematics. . . . It's *the* story of our time." It is also
implausibly conceived: science and math prodigies are generally known to manifest and pursue their gifts very early, proceeding in concentrated unipolar fashion. But what Trilling was
after — to accommodate his plot and its anticipated climax —
was some mammoth all-encompassing persona, a type of muscular masculinity steeped in lasting fame: he would have such
a man turn imprudently wild in consequence of a reckless obsession with a young girl four decades his junior. Trilling's real-
life model, he informs us, was at first Walter Savage Landor, a
nineteenth-century English poet "of heroic size," similarly infatuated in old age. Yet Buxton as he develops (insofar as he is
developed at all) is closer to an amalgam of William James, the
scientist-adventurer, and Henry James, the closeted imaginer —
on whom Trilling purposefully bestows a robust heterosexual
lust. (Or so Professor Murphy acutely parses it.)

That Outram should choose an unseasoned twenty-three-
year-old, evidently talented but lacking any literary standing,
for this daunting biographical project — an interpretive likeness
of a man "weighty with years, wisdom, power" — is a puzzle.
It will not occur to Vincent until much later in the progress of
the narrative to suspect Outram of a clandestine motive for so
grand an anomaly, and the novel breaks off before any such motive is revealed. In the meantime, Vincent is catapulted into a
sophisticated circle light years from his shabby midwestern ori-

gins. In the cultivated interiors and environs of Harold and May Outram's home, situated "in a New England town of considerable tradition," he is introduced to a series of half-explained persons, all deeply implicated with one another in ways not immediately apparent. The cumulative effect of these characters as they enter their respective scenes singly or in clusters is reminiscent of those familiar Hollywood whodunits where all the likely suspects, each with a reasonable alibi, are assembled for interrogation by a shrewdly knowing investigator. Vincent, however, is not shrewd; he is intelligent and alert, though still youthfully uncomprehending, and always tagged with variations of the epithets of incompleteness Trilling tirelessly attaches to him: "so immature and inexperienced," "waiting for things to happen to him," "like a foreigner in a new land," "the various perils which beset the young man who gives himself to the life of the mind," "with how many attempts to master its own inchoateness would this young mind of his move," "he was a young man who thought much of fame, power, and success in life," and on and on.

In this cloud of unknowing, the emphatically untried Vincent is made to confront a formidably bearded Jorris Buxton, an octogenarian who turns out to be frightened by a thunderstorm; his inscrutable assistant, Brooks Barrett; Garda Thorne, a middle-aged short story writer of some renown, who at seventeen was mistress to Buxton, then fifty-five (her name purloined from a novel by Constance Fenimore Woolson, a Henry James connection); Linda and Arthur Hollowell, a wealthy couple eager to buy a school to further their social views; Philip Dyas, the school's headmaster, reluctant to sell; Marion Cathcart, the Outram children's young caretaker, to whom Buxton appears attracted; and Claudine Post, whose infantilized teenage charge, Perdita, is described as being in a "not harmless" relation to Buxton.

It is a crowded gallery of carefully delineated portraits, whose innerness is divulged partly through dialogue but far more extensively in passages of cannily analyzed insight. And like pictures on a wall, it is all static—inevitably so, to begin with, since the problem of the story (every story implies a problem) is still undefined when the novel is cut short. Also, it should not be forgotten that the manuscript Professor Murphy unearthed was a draft in formation. The crucial proof of this middle-of-the-journey uncertainty is an appendix she has titled "Trilling's Commentary," yet another overview of the novelist's intentions. There are self-admonitory reminders such as "the chapter should glitter more," "make the likelihood of the choice of Vincent the greater and also the more acceptable," and "what is making the difficulty is that I have not yet got a new point at which to aim." Despite these strictures and doubts, Trilling's narrative skill is now and then on bright display, especially in the earliest chapters touching on Vincent's childhood and adolescent friendship with a boy whom Vincent will ultimately outgrow intellectually. Toss Dodge is the little boy who has just moved into the neighborhood:

Vincent stood on his part of the sidewalk and looked at the newcomer, who looked back and then turned his attention to the moving-men. Vincent kicked his way over to the curb and examined something at the edge of the road. He looked at it with a deep, rather amused curiosity. He touched it with the toe of his shoe. The object, whatever it was, engaged his attention as a Naturalist, a person to whom all things were significant. Actually he was examining nothing at all. But to justify his attention, he picked up a fallen seed-pod, peered at it a moment with a discerning eye, then threw it away. . . .

Meanwhile Toss had taken a position of responsibility near the van. He stood with his hands behind his back, supervising with quiet vigilance the operations of his men. He said nothing but he was sharp-sighted and a slight frown showed that he was not to be imposed on by his subordinates.

They were both now established in sufficient importance and could acknowledge each other.

Vincent said, "Hello," carelessly, take it or leave it.

Toss answered in kind.

"You moving in?" said Vincent.

"Uh-huh. You live here?"

This is a mastery of boyhood worthy of Mark Twain. Nor was Trilling unaware of the intuitiveness through which it was consummated. "The first part," he confirmed, "did grow into something. And it grew with a kind of unconsciousness. This unconsciousness was very beguiling and reassuring." It will not often recur in the remainder of the narrative. Trilling's habit of theorizing perceptiveness ordinarily overrides the Keatsian negative capability he so much reveres — that openness to the oarless vagaries of the mind he regularly invokes in the essays. Yet the beguiling and reassuring intervals did come. Sentence by sentence, in striking set pieces and in short breaths and long,

the freed imagination at times felicitously crops up — a staccato phrase here, a winding image there: wild flowers peeping
through monuments of sculptured topiary. One such specimen,
visual and tactile, is Buxton's beard:

> It was the best kind of beard that a man can wear, it was short
> and firm and jutted forward. It gave a base to the head and did
> not mask the face. It suggested fortitude and the possibility of
> just anger. ... No one had happened to mention to [Vincent]
> that Jorris Buxton wore a beard. Out of the haze of other peo-
> ple's attitudes this immediate fact emerged with a happy, bris-
> tly reality.

But this happy, bristly reality, impulsively observed and
weighed, is too soon dowsed by metaphysics. Trilling is almost
never sufficiently free of the burden, or the constriction, of understanding a character too well — even before that character
is moved into action or speech. What ought to have been viv-
idly revelatory — the force of the great man's spirit when at last
he sits down with his biographer — is somehow deflected into
humdrum brooding discursiveness. Its immediate ground is the
intrusive presence of Buxton's servile assistant, whose "striking
repulsiveness" Buxton mutely erases through a kind of contem-
plative transcendence, sweeping Vincent into what purports to
be sudden feeling:

> Vincent tried to give words to the emotion he felt. It was, he
> could say, the emotion of pure disinterestedness. ... Vincent
> made use of the word "pure" because that word suggested the
> sensation of crystalline, translucent being that he had felt. He

eventually hit upon another word, "peace," remarking that what was probably meant by that word was a perfect poise of energies without the alloy of personality. He reminded himself that the ancient philosophers, when they spoke so passionately to recommend death, probably had these conditions in mind. They obviously could not mean non-existence. They must have meant an existence in perfect equilibrium of the impulses and powers with no element of that greed which they identified as the personality. This condition of being was sometimes permitted by life, but life was always presenting demands that brought the experience to an end. Hence, Vincent supposed, the recommendation of death.

Death, yes! Deadly prose, dead on the page. Where is Buxton in all this? Where, as a matter of fact, is Vincent, through whom these cerebrations course? The beard is *written;* the beard is alive; the beard is a character in a novel. But Buxton has vanished, and Vincent himself recedes behind the privet hedge of abstraction. The fault is not that Trilling's recitation here deals solely with ideas, and not so much that it is repetitively clotted, and not even that it eschews drama. Thought *as* drama, the act of thinking as a vehicle of high excitement, is anyhow central to Trilling's credo. Vincent's story, the authorial preface points out, "is of a kind that will inevitably throw off ideas; and the characters are articulate, intelligent, and embody certain moralities." Then why does the novel fail—fatally—in this crucial first encounter between its two supposedly articulate and intelligent major figures? Novels—great novels—are known to be studded with meditative insertions that not only do not produce longueurs, they leave behind traces of glory.

Dostoyevsky's Grand Inquisitor may be too heatedly elevated an instance; but think of James's Isabel Archer, alone and motionless before the fire, sunk in rumination for twenty uninterrupted pages. *The Portrait of a Lady* can sustain this dialogueless island of inaction because it is preceded and followed by everything that a novel is and does to seduce us into feeling it is alive.

Trilling's refusal — or his inability — to allow Buxton to speak at the very juncture it is most urgent for him to speak collapses what is to come. Or, rather, he does speak, he is said to speak, but we cannot hear him. It isn't enough for Vincent to send out signals or symptoms of Buxton's thought: "the eyes lived with the life of the contemplating mind ... the eyes showed, or so Vincent felt, a life beyond the words that Buxton was speaking." But this is dumbshow, a silent movie — where *are* the words? The snatches of Buxton's talk scattered through the few remaining chapters are no more than mannerly clues on the style of "show them in," "do sit down," "a fine bunch of a girl," and one or two meager remarks on Darwin. Vincent can insist, on one occasion or another, that "in whatever way Buxton judged what he saw, he certainly saw a great deal," and still the reassurance will instantly wither. What Buxton sees we cannot see. What Buxton feels we cannot feel. Buxton has no voice and no movement. Buxton is dead; a wraith.

Perhaps Trilling knew it. He knew what his novel was made of. It would be wrong and unfair, even brutal, to say, as many have said, that he was too intelligent to succeed at fiction, which courts fancy more than reason. After all, he had the conditions and trappings of a novel; he had its language, masterly and penetrating; he had the novel's shape and its emotional furnishings;

he had the different tenors of his intellect, its analytic capacity
and its deep historical wisdom. He had his spurts of beguile-
ment. He had, in short, all the equipment for the engineering
of a novel. Yet he must have felt, finally, that he also had a dead
man on his hands. Worse, in the end he took himself to be a
simulacrum of that man. At fifty-seven, long after he had abandoned what was to have been his second novel, he lamented in
his journal, "Nothing has so filled me with shame and regret as
what I have not done." He had not become what he hoped to be:
a novelist commanding, authentic, and recognized. Instead, he
had turned into his own Teddy Kramer, that enervated effigy of
"Jewish pride," a creature of such scrupulous intellectual honesty that he could not bring the longed-for work to a satisfactory
conclusion.

And why was it imperative to write novels? "In my time,"
Outram, who gave up fiction for social influence, ruefully tells
Vincent, "it was novel or nothing." Outram speaks for Trilling:
in his time, novel or nothing. Then was that resplendent body
of literary and cultural essays, and the university, and the authority, and the fame, and ultimately the legend — was all that
nothing?

The Lastingness of Saul Bellow

How easy it is, and plausible, to regard a collection of letters spanning youth and old age as an approximation of autobiography: the procession of denizens who inhabit a life, the bit players with their entrances and exits, the faithful chronology of incidents — all turn up reliably in either form, whether dated and posted or backward-looking. Yet autobiography, even when ostensibly steeped in candor, tends toward reconsideration — if not revisionary paperings-over, then late perspectives and second thoughts. Whereas letters (but here let us specify a *writer's* letters) are appetite and urgency, unmediated seizures of impulse and desire torn from the fraught and living moment. And letters — sorted, indexed, bound — are themselves a paradox: hotly alive, they claim death as a requisite. Rare and anomalous is the publisher who would prefer the correspondence of the quick, however celebrated, to the letters of the dead: the death of a writer who answers his mail, especially one possessed of a powerful fame, lengthens and amplifies the body of work.

Even so, death disports with writers more cruelly than with the rest of humankind. The grave can hardly make more mute those who were voiceless when alive — dust to dust, muteness to muteness. But the silence that dogs the established writer's noisy obituary, with its boisterous shock and busy regret, is more profound than any other. Oblivion comes more cuttingly to the writer whose presence has been *felt,* argued over, championed, disparaged — the writer who is seen to be what Lionel Trilling calls a Figure. *Lionel Trilling?* Consider: who at this hour (apart from some professorial specialist currying his "field") is reading Mary McCarthy, James T. Farrell, John Berryman, Allan Bloom, Irving Howe, Alfred Kazin, Edmund Wilson, Anne Sexton, Alice Adams, Robert Lowell, Grace Paley, Owen Barfield, Stanley Elkin, Robert Penn Warren, Norman Mailer, Leslie Fiedler, R. P. Blackmur, Paul Goodman, Susan Sontag, Lillian Hellman, John Crowe Ransom, Stephen Spender, Daniel Fuchs, Hugh Kenner, Seymour Krim, J. F. Powers, Allen Ginsberg, Philip Rahv, Jack Richardson, John Auerbach, Harvey Swados — or Trilling himself? These names of the dead — a good number of them past luminaries, a few (Lillian Hellman, say) worthy of being forgotten — do not come randomly. They all have their fleeting turn in Saul Bellow's letters, whether vituperatively, casually, or approvingly (though scarcely ever indifferently). It is safe to say that most are nowadays not much in demand either at your local library or on Amazon, and safer yet to surmise that many have little chance of outlasting even the first third of the twenty-first century; several have barely outlasted the twentieth. Nearly all have been overtaken by newer writers lately grown familiar, vernal aspirants who crowd the horizon with their addictive clamor.

And even as these contemporary importunings swamp our perception, what can already be clearly discerned rising from this swelling armada of the twice-buried is a single exemption: Bellow. Among all the literary tumults and public roilings of the recently Famous, he alone courts lastingness, he alone escapes eclipse. To state this so bluntly is not so much a declaration as it is an inquiry. Only see how speedily the grave works its mufflings and comedowns — Ginsberg, mum; Mailer, dumb as stone. In the tracings of unassailable art, high or low, they leave improbable spoor: the poet no poet but minstrel and mountebank, the would-be immortal novelist undone by the politicized harlequin he became. Gradually they decay into symptom and artifact — documents of a receding social history — while the vestigial rustlings surrounding their names testify to nothing more memorable than outdated literary tinsel.

But Bellow stays, and why? Language — the acclaimed style — cannot be the whole of it, though its energetic capaciousness captures and capsizes American English with an amplitude and verve not heard since Whitman, and never before in prose. The mandarin-poolroom link, elevated riffs married to street vernacular, has become Bellow's signature, and attracts lovestruck imitators. Yet brilliant flourishes alone, even when embedded in galloping ambition, will not make a second Bellow. (A second Bellow? Not for a hundred years!) There is instead something else, beyond the heated braininess and lavish command of ideas: call it *feeling*. In this bountiful volume of letters, the writer's last brief words, set down fourteen months before his death, should all at once break open the hidden-in-plain-sight code that reveals why Bellow stays:

[My parents] needed all the help they could get. They were forever asking, "What does the man say?" and I would translate for them into heavy-footed English. The old people were as ignorant of English as they were of Canadian French. We often stopped before a display of children's shoes. My mother coveted for me a pair of patent-leather sandals with an *elegantissimo* strap. I finally got them — I rubbed them with butter to preserve the leather. This is when I was six or seven years old. . . . Amazing how it all boils down to a pair of patent-leather sandals.

It all boils down to a pair of patent-leather sandals. A dying old man's sentimental nostalgia, a fruitlessly self-indulgent yearning for a mother lost too soon? No; or not only. What we are hearing also is the culmination of a theory of pastness — and pastness means passage. In nine sentences, an annotated history of an immigrant family, where it settled, how it struggled, how it aspired; and a hint of the future novelist's moral aesthetic, the determination to preserve. As with the family, so with the family of man. Bellow, who as a graduate student studied anthropology, as a writer pursues the history of civilized thought — an inquisitiveness directed to the way experience (Augie) turns into a quest for philosophy (Henderson, Sammler, Herzog), sometimes via a scalding bath of comedy.

The letters are all zest and craving and demand — so many journeys, so many cities, so many liaisons, so many courtings, so many marriages and partings, so many spasms of rage, so many victories and downers, so many blue or frenetic melancholias and grievances; but cumulatively they add up to a rich montage of knowing, speckled now and again with laughter, that most metaphysical of emotions. And always, pulsing below the hungry race, the loyalty to pastness. Well into Bellow's old age, Chicago's Tuley High School held an emblematic place in his psyche. Tuley was where the excitations of intellectual ambition first encountered their kin in the formidably intelligent children of mostly working-class immigrant Jews, boys and girls drenched in ferocious bookishness and utopian politics, unselfconsciously asserting ownership of American culture at a time when it was most vigorously dominated by WASPs. Nathan Gould, Louis Lasco, Oscar Tarcov, David Peltz, Stuart Brent, Herbert Passin, Abe Kaufman, Hymen Slate, Louis Sidran, Rosalyn Tureck, Zita Cogan, Yetta Barshevsky, Sam Freifeld, and especially Isaac Rosenfeld — Bellow kept up with a surprising number of these witnesses to his early ardors, and mourned acutely when the dying of old friends began. In a letter to Nathan Gould in 1981, the Nobel five years behind him, he fell into elegy:

> I attended the Tuley reunion and it was a depressing affair — elderly people nostalgic for youth and the Depression years. There seemed nothing for them (for us) to do but turn into middle-class Americans with the same phrases and thoughts from the same sources. Some came from far away . . . and some were crippled and required wheeling. . . . [One] who seemed well preserved turned out to have a heredity disorder affecting his memory so that he was groping, while we talked, and his new wife was deeply uneasy. . . . But my closest friends were Oscar and Isaac, dead for many years. In every decade I try to think what they might have been had they lived.

He ended with a tribute to "the old days." If as "a sort of public man" he didn't retain the old affections, he said, "I would feel alienated from my own history, *false.*"

Fifteen years later, at a memorial service for Yetta Barshevsky, who had been Tuley's class orator and radical firebrand, elegy burst into exuberant reminiscence. After reciting Yetta's street address of seven decades before (and his own, "right around the corner"), after dismissing her "spectacularly handsome" mother as an unregenerate Stalinist and describing her carpenter father's "jalopy . . . filled with saws and sawdust," he appended a tour de force of recollection:

> I even came to know Yetta's grandfather, whom I often saw at the synagogue when I came to say Kaddish for my mother. He was an extremely, primitively orthodox short bent man with a beard that seemed to rush out of him and muffled his face. He wore a bowler hat and elastic-sided boots. The old women, it seems, were wildly radical communist sympathizers. The grandfathers were the pious ones.

Passages like these, with their sociohistorical notation and their indelible optical prowess — rushing beard, elastic-sided boots! — can easily be found reverberating in any of Bellow's stories and novels. And even in the very first letter in this collection, a clowning response to Yetta's having jilted him in favor of one Nathan Goldstein, Bellow at seventeen was already a conscious writer — antic, teasing, showing off, pumping adolescent brio and witty pastiche. He *felt* what he was; he was sure of what he had. Like Henry James and T. S. Eliot, those confident conquistadors of London who were his precursors in early self-knowledge, Bellow claimed recognition before he was in a position to have earned it. But London was an insular village vulnerable to conquest, and America was a continent. What could be accomplished gracefully, if cattily, in Virginia Woolf's Tavistock Square required boldness in Chicago.

In 1932, Bellow is a teenage boy writing to a teenage girl; five years on, as subeditor of an obscure Trotskyist journal, he addresses James T. Farrell in the worldly tones of a seasoned colleague — though at twenty-two he has so far published only occasional pieces. "It is peculiar," Bellow instructs Farrell, who had become his mentor, "how the Stalinites have lost central discipline by spreading themselves through liberal groups.... [Sydney] Harris thinks nothing of assassinating a scruple or knifing a principle if thereby he can profit." This fierce disparagement — the skewering of a now nearly forgotten journalist in that antediluvian period when "Trotskyist" and "Stalinite" were warring bywords — only intensified as Bellow aged into viewpoints adversarial to his youthful radicalism. In 1986, summing up for Karl Shapiro his impressions of an international writers' congress in New York sponsored by PEN, he dismissed a clutch of contemporary notables: "Mailer," he reported, "mostly wanted a huge media event — that's what he calls living.... It boggled my mind to see how greedy the radicals were for excitement 'radical-style.' I'm speaking of big-time subversives like Ginsberg, Nadine Gordimer, Grace Paley, Doctorow, and other representatives of affluent revolution." One can marvel at how the polemical voice of the mature Bellow is scarcely changed (despite the change of politics) from that of the self-

assured and strenuously contentious young man of fifty years
before — yet even more striking is how Bellow in his twenties
is ready to pit his taste and his talent against anyone, however
more established. To be famous and forceful at seventy is one
thing; to believe in one's fame before it has evolved is a kind
of magical faith. It was an authority — no, an authenticity —
that carried him far. He had no intention (so the letters reveal)
of wasting time as a novitiate pursuing deferential cultivation
of influential eminences. His approach was that of an instant
equal. His successful candidacy (and third try) for a Guggenheim fellowship elicited support from Farrell, Edmund Wilson, and Robert Penn Warren. He had already been in friendly
correspondence with all three, and was intimate enough with
Warren to know him as "Red."

Still earlier, he had quickly formed a connection with Philip
Rahv of *Partisan Review,* the most imperially prestigious literary magnet of the Forties. For the young Bellow, publication
failed to satisfy if it fell short of widening both courage and opportunity. James Henle of Vanguard Press, who in 1944 brought
out *Dangling Man,* Bellow's first published novel — later followed by *The Victim* — was soon jettisoned. To Henry Volken-
ing, his agent, Bellow spoke of "swollen feelings," and to Henle
he wrote sourly:

> I know you will accuse me again of putting off the philosopher's
> robe and of being too impatient, and that you will repeat that
> before I have published five or six books I can't expect to live
> by writing. But as I write slowly I will be forty before my fifth
> book is ready and I don't think it is unreasonable of me to ex-

pect that the most should be made of what I do produce. When
I see my chances for uninterrupted work going down the drain
I can't help protesting the injustice of it. This year I have been
ill and teaching leaves me no energy for writing. [Bellow at this
time was assistant professor of English at the University of Min-
nesota.] . . . I see next year and the next and the one after that
fribbled away at the university. My grievance is a legitimate one,
I think. I don't want to be a commercial writer or to be taken
up with money. I have never discussed money matters with you
in four years, except for the letter I wrote you last spring about
[*The Victim*]. You were annoyed with me. . . . But now the book
is out, it hasn't been badly received and already it seems to be
going the way of *Dangling Man*. ·

The letter was not sent. But the break with Henle was carried out; it stood for more than ambition, more than a writer's
nervous self-advocacy. It was clairvoyance, it was a heralding,
it spoke for the cause of imagination untrammeled. Already it
bristled with the thickening future. His second novel only just
published, Bellow was numbering the long row of still-to-be-
written novels ahead. The unsent letter was not about money —
it was about freedom, it was about becoming. Even more, it
was about knowing. Bellow knew what he knew, and like some
youthfully anointed evangelist, he wanted what he knew to be
known. The flight from Henle was the beginning of a credo.

And what was that credo? An impulse running through many
of the letters discloses it: it was, plainly and unaffectedly, how
to *see;* meaning, at bottom, how a novelist must think. For decades it has been common wisdom — common because Bellow

himself made it so—that *Dangling Man* and *The Victim,* the pair of novels preceding *The Adventures of Augie March,* were too "Flaubertian," too controlled, pinched by the orderliness of European modernist constraint, while *Augie* was an extravagant release into the impetuous comedic buoyancy of a manifold America. Of *The Victim,* Bellow was moved to write:

> Compared to what is published nowadays between boards, it is an accomplishment. By my own standards, however, it is promissory. It took hold of my mind and imagination very deeply but I know that I somehow failed to write it *freely,* with all the stops out from beginning to end.... And I must admit that in spite of the great amount of energy I brought to the book at certain times, I was at others, for some reason, content to fall back on lesser resources.... But there is a certain diffidence about me ... that prevents me from going all out.... I assemble the dynamite but I am not ready to touch off the fuse. Why? Because I am working toward something and have not arrived....
> I wanted to write before I had the maturity to write as "high" as I wished and so I had a very arduous and painful apprenticeship and am still undergoing it.

Or so he declared in January 1948. But by April he was disputing this unforgiving verdict, complaining of "a rather disagreeable letter from Kurt [Wolff] about *The Victim.* I didn't mind his criticisms of specific things but I disliked extremely his telling me 'you aren't there *yet.*'" *The Victim,* he went on, "is a powerful book.... There aren't many recent books that come close to it and I can't take seriously any opinion that doesn't begin by acknowledging that." Adding more than sixty years of reappraisal to Bellow's spare three months, we can argue even more effectively against the notion of apprenticeship. There is by now no getting away from it: the earlier novels need not, should not, be overshadowed or diminished by *Augie*. It is not too daring to venture that if *Augie* — grand gusts of vitality notwithstanding — had never come into being, Bellow would still have been Bellow: the mind, the wit, the word, the reach; the perplexity and the delirium of the human animal. There are whole pages in *Dangling Man* that might have been torn out of *Seize the Day*. There are rolling tracts of dialogue in *The Victim* with telling affinities to *Ravelstein*. The familiar metaphysical cunning is everywhere. From the start, Bellow wrote "high." And the key to writing high, said this most intellectual of novelists, is to force intellect into hiding, to trick the explicit into vanishing into the implicit.

To Leslie Fiedler, who accused him of "misology" — hatred of argument and reason — he recited his unwavering principle of elasticity:

> I think positions *emerge* in a work of art, and you seem to think they're imposed. It makes small difference what the artist says he thinks, and a "prepared" attitude is an invitation to disaster. . . . I only complain that intelligence has become so naked.

And to Josephine Herbst:

> If you think *Seize the Day* is good, I'm satisfied that I'm doing all right. It's hard for me to know, because so much of the time I'm deaf, dumb and blind, the slave of unknown masters.

To John Berryman:

> All the formal properties have to be cracked and the simplicities released.

To Ruth Miller, who had sent him her essay on Ralph Ellison's *Invisible Man:*

> Your explication is too dense, too detailed. . . . Perhaps it is too much like laboratory analysis. . . . You see, you have left out the literary side of the matter almost entirely, and that, to my mind, is a mistake. I myself distinguish between the parts of the novel that were *written* and those that were constructed as part of the argument; they are not alike in quality . . . your interest is in Opinion rather than Creation.

To the Guggenheim Foundation, in support of Bernard Malamud's application for a fellowship:

> Imagination has been steadily losing prestige in American life, it seems to me, for a long time. I am speaking of the poetic imagination. Inferior kinds of imagination have prospered, but the poetic has less credit than ever before. Perhaps that is because there is less room than ever for the personal, the spacious, unanxious and free, for the unprepared, unorganized, and spontaneous elements from which poetic imagination springs.

To Louis Gallo, while working on *Herzog:*

> You'll find the book I'm writing now less "tender," "tolerant," etc. When a writer has such feelings, however, it's his business to lead them all into the hottest fire. He must expose them to the

most destructive opposites he can find and, if he wishes to be
tender, confront the murderer's face. The converse, however,
is equally true, for writers who believe there is a Sargasso of
vomit into which we must drift are obliged to confront beauty.
To deny that, you would have to deny your instincts as a writer.

To Robert Penn Warren:

Augie was very difficult for me in the last half. I suppose I succumbed to the dreadful thing I warn everyone against — seriousness. . . . My slogan was "Easily or not at all," but I forgot it.
Too much of a temptation to speak the last word.

To Susan Glassman:

Somehow I've managed to do exactly what I like. There are certain philosophers (Samuel Butler, if he is one) who say we really
do get what we want. Question: Can we bear it when we get it?
That's the question that's the beginning of religion.

To Richard Stern:

No amount of assertion will make an ounce of art.

But he did assert his *idea* of art — he asserted his instincts,
his intuitions — and he did do exactly what he liked, at least
in everything he wrote, and he really did get what he wanted,
if not sooner, then later. His sovereignty as a writer was, so to
say, *built in*. And for every statement of credo-instruction, especially when directed to other writers, he appended generous
tributes. When he was stirred to criticism, he almost always began with self-criticism, taking on himself the very flaw he had

fingered in the other. There might be an occasional exception, most particularly if the object of scrutiny was a fellow novelist publicly acknowledged to be on his own team. With such confirmed colleagues he pulled no punches: he wrote scathingly to Philip Roth, disparaging *I Married a Communist* and lecturing him on Stalin's Western loyalists and "hatred of one's own country." He was merciless toward Malamud's *A New Life:* "all the middle-class platitudes of love and liberalism . . . mean and humorless." Nevertheless there was personal warmth and varying degrees of literary admiration for his confederates in the triumvirate he parodied as "Hart, Schaffner and Marx," a quip that has survived the decades. What reluctantly united all three — Bellow, Roth, Malamud — was a concept imposed on them by the celebrity-sloganeering of the journalists: "American Jewish writers." But the link was both superficial and specious: each invented his own mythos and imagined his own republic of letters. It was not the complexity of heritage Bellow was resisting in his tailor-made mockery, but its reduction to a narrowing palliative, nowadays fashionably termed "identity." In a memorial tribute to Malamud, Bellow reiterated his ties to the old atmospherics of origins, while introducing a still greater claim:

> We were cats of the same breed. The sons of Eastern European immigrant Jews, we had gone early into the streets of our respective cities, were Americanized by schools, newspapers, subways, streetcars, sandlots. Melting Pot children, we had assumed the American program to be the real thing: no barriers to the freest and fullest American choices. Of course we understood that it was no simple civics-course matter. We knew too

much about the slums, we had assimilated too much dark history in our mothers' kitchens to be radiant optimists . . . it was admiration, it was love that drew us to the dazzling company of the great masters, all of them belonging to the Protestant Majority — some of them explicitly anti-Semitic. . . . But one could not submit to control by such prejudices. My own view was that in religion the Christians had lived with us, had lived in the Bible of the Jews, but when the Jews wished to live in Western history with them they were refused. As if that history was not, by now, also ours.

These words (brilliantly included among the letters) were recited on Bellow's behalf under the dim chandeliers of the meeting room of the American Academy of Arts and Letters, where the members' chairs bore brass plaques inscribed with such storied names as Henry Adams, Owen Wister, Hamlin Garland, Edwin Markham, and other venerable representatives of Bellow's capitalized Majority. And when, not yet out of their teens, he and Isaac Rosenfeld dissolved the solemn ironies of Eliot's "Love Song of J. Alfred Prufrock" into a hilariously lampooning Yiddish ditty, it may have marked the signal moment when writers born Jewish and awakened into America would refuse to be refused by Western history.

Bellow's capacity for what might (in quick march) be called Jewish intelligence summoned deeps far beyond where the journalists could follow: the literary talent that rose up, in puzzling if impressive flocks, out of what appeared to be a low immigrant culture. Bellow was distinctive in transcending — transgressing against — the archetype of the coarse and unlettered ghetto greenhorn. The greenhorns in their humble trades were aware that they were carriers of a moral civilization. ("You are too intelligent for this," Herzog protests to his vaporously overtheorizing friend Shapiro. "Your father had rich blood. He peddled apples.") Though he had repeatedly declared himself, as an American, free to choose according to will or desire, Bellow also chose not to be disaffected. He was in possession of an inherited literacy that few novelists of Jewish background, writers of or close to his generation, could match, however sophisticated otherwise they might be. His range spanned an inclusive continuum; as his eulogy for Malamud insisted, Western learning and literature had also to mean Jewish learning and literature. He was at home in biblical Hebrew, was initiated into the liturgy from early childhood, and read and spoke (always with relish) a supple Yiddish. In the letters he will now and again slide into a Yiddish word or phrase for its pungent or familial aptness where English might pale. It was Bellow who, with Irving Howe and the Yiddish poet Eliezer Greenberg standing by, translated I. B. Singer's "Gimpel the Fool," in effect creating, in a matter of hours, a modernist American writer out of what had passed, mistakenly, for an old-fashioned Yiddish storyteller. What other "American Jewish writer" could have pulled off this feat? Or would have been willing to set aside the mask of fiction to pursue — his personal viewpoint plain to see — the political culture of Israel, as Bellow did in *To Jerusalem and Back*, a book-length essay composed at the crux of churning contention? (Decades old and read today, it remains, in its candor and credibility, shatteringly up-to-date.) And finally — we are compelled to come to this — there is the strangely misunderstood question of Bellow and the Holocaust.

In a letter dated July 19, 1987, he wrote:

It's perfectly true that "Jewish writers in America" (a repulsive category!) missed what should have been for them the central event of their time, the destruction of European Jewry. We (I speak of Jews now and not merely writers) should have reckoned more fully, more deeply with it. . . . I was too busy becoming a novelist to take note of what was happening in the Forties. I was involved with "literature" and given over to preoccupations with art, with language, with my struggle on the American scene, with the claims for recognition of my talent or, like my pals at the *Partisan Review,* with modernism, Marxism, New Criticism, with Eliot, Yeats, Proust, etc.—with anything except the terrible events in Poland. Growing slowly aware of this unspeakable evasion I didn't even know how to begin to admit it into my inner life. Not a particle of this can be denied. And can I really say—can anyone say—what was to be done, how this "thing" ought to have been met? Since the late Forties I have been brooding about it and sometimes I imagine I *can* see something. But what brooding may amount to is probably insignificant. I can't even begin to say what responsibility any of us may bear in such a matter, a crime so vast that it brings all Being into Judgment.

If there appears to be a contradiction in this arresting statement, it is hardly to the point. "I was too busy becoming a novelist to take note of what was happening in the Forties" may in fact clash with "Since the late Forties I have been brooding about it," but it is the closing phrase that calls reality into question—the known reality of "the terrible events in Poland." Bellow was made fully aware of these events earlier than most, and

with a close-up precision unbefogged by such grand metaphorical abstractions as "a crime so vast that it brings all Being into
Judgment." The writer who could explicitly describe the particular texture of an old man's boots glimpsed seventy years before
here fades into the elusiveness of high declamation. Yet a single
much-overlooked biographical datum may dispute these asser-
tions of overriding literary distraction. In 1948, three years after
the defeat of Germany and the appalling revelations of the death
camps, Bellow and Anita Goshkin, the social worker who became his first wife, went with their small son Gregory to live in
Paris; a Guggenheim grant made the move possible. Bellow settled in to work on a new novel, caught up in the convivial cadres of literary Americans drawn to postwar Paris, while Anita
found a job with the Joint Distribution Committee. Here we
must pause to take this in. The Joint, as it was called, was a privately funded American effort to salvage the broken lives of the
remnant of Holocaust survivors; Anita was perforce immersed
daily in freshly accumulating news of "the terrible events in Poland." Are we to believe that the wife never imparted to the husband what she learned and witnessed and felt every day, or that,
detached, he took no notice of it?

But if we may not conjecture what a wife privately recounts to
a husband — even one so alert to the historically momentous —
the letters themselves, with their multiple sharp retrospections,
are testimony enough. In 1978, writing to the twenty-something
Leon Wieseltier ("I found I could tell you things"), Bellow re-
sponded to a pair of articles Wieseltier had sent him on the phil-
osophic origins of Hannah Arendt's post-Holocaust thinking.
"That superior Krautess," as Bellow dubbed her, had notori-

ously charged the European Jewish leadership with collabora-
tion in the administration of the Nazi ghettos and deportations.
"She could often think clearly," Bellow tells Wieseltier, "but to
think simply was altogether beyond her, and her imaginative
faculty was stunted." He goes on to cite the "simple facts":

> I once asked Alexander Donat, author of *The Holocaust King-
> dom,* how it was that the Jews went down so quickly in Poland.
> He said something like this: "After three days in the ghetto,
> unable to wash and shave, without clean clothing, deprived
> of food, all utilities and municipal services cut off, your toilet
> habits humiliatingly disrupted, you are demoralized, confused,
> subject to panic. A life of austere discipline would have made it
> possible to keep my head, but how many civilized people had
> such a life?" Such simple facts—had Hannah had the imagina-
> tion to see them—would have vitiated her theories.

Arendt may have been a respectable if not wholly respected
adversary, but the treasonous Ezra Pound was likely the most
poisonous figure by whom Bellow judged both "the terrible
events in Poland" and the writers who declined to face them.
In 1982, addressing Robert Boyers's commiseration with what
Boyers termed an "uncharitable" review of *The Dean's December* by the critic Hugh Kenner, Bellow fulminated against Kenner's "having come out openly in his Eliot-Pound anti-Semitic
regalia" in defense of Pound. Infamous for his wartime broad-
casts from Mussolini's Italy—tirade after tirade on Jews and
"usury"—Pound had nevertheless attracted faithful literary
champions. "It was that the poet's convictions could be sepa-
rated from his poetry," Bellow argued. "It was thus possible to

segregate the glory from the shame. Then you took possession of the glory in the name of 'culture' and kept the malignancies as a pet." A quarter of a century before, in 1956, in the most coldly furious confrontation to be found here, Bellow had already accused William Faulkner of heartlessly overlooking Pound's malevolence. As head of a presidentially appointed committee of writers "to promote pro-American values abroad," Faulkner had asked Bellow to sign on to a recommendation for Pound's release from his confinement in a hospital for the insane; though deemed a traitor, he had been spared prison. With uncommon bitterness, Bellow retorted:

> Pound advocated in his poems and in his broadcasts enmity to the Jews and preached hatred and murder. Do you mean to ask me to join you in honoring a man who called for the destruction of my kinsmen? I can take no part in such a thing even if it makes effective propaganda abroad, which I doubt. Europeans will take it instead as a symptom of reaction. In France, Pound would have been shot. Free him because he is a poet? Why, better poets than he were exterminated perhaps.
>
> Shall we say nothing in their behalf? America has dealt mercifully with Pound in sparing his life. To release him is a feeble and foolish idea. It would identify this program in the eyes of the world with Hitler and Himmler and Mussolini and genocide. . . . What staggers me is that you and Mr. [John] Steinbeck who have dealt for so many years in words should fail to understand the import of Ezra Pound's plain and brutal statements about the "kikes" leading the "goy" to slaughter. Is this — from *The Pisan Cantos* — the stuff of poetry? It is a call to murder. . . . The whole world conspires to ignore what has happened, the

giant wars, the colossal hatreds, the unimaginable murders, the destruction of the very image of man. And we — "a representative group of American writers" — is this what we come out for, too?

In light of this uncompromising cri de coeur, and of similar mordant reflections in the novels and stories (covertly in *The Victim* and boldly elsewhere), how are we to regard Bellow's "I was too busy becoming a novelist" apologia? A false note: there was, in fact, no "unspeakable evasion"; rather, an enduring recognition of acid shame and remorse. *And can I really say — can anyone say — what was to be done?* Clearly, and from the first, he saw and he knew.

Now it may be imagined — or even insisted — that too much is being made of all this, that the emphasis here is disproportionate, and that there are other dimensions, more conspicuous and profuse, which can more readily define Bellow as writer. Or it can be said, justifiably, that he openly denigrated anything resembling special pleading — after all, hadn't he brushed off as "a repulsive category" the phrase "Jewish writers in America"? And what was this dismissal if not a repudiation of a vulgarizing tendency to bypass the art in order to laud the artist as a kind of ethnic cheerleader — much as young Jewish baseball fans are encouraged to look to Hank Greenberg for prideful self-validation. Besides, he had long ago put himself on record as freewheeling, unfettered, unprescribed, liberated from direction or coercion. In words that will not be found in the correspondence (they derive from the essays, those publicly personal letters to readers), Bellow wrote, "I would not allow myself to become the product of an *environment*" — flaunting willful italics. And though he never failed to refresh his law of the unleashed life, it rang now with a decisive coda: "In my generation, the children of immigrants *became* American. An effort was required. One made oneself, freestyle. . . . I was already an American, and I was also a Jew. I had an American outlook, superadded to a Jewish consciousness." To Faulkner's indifference he could speak — powerfully, inexorably — of "my kinsmen." And to history the same.

Say, then, that he was, as he intended to be, free, unstinting in what he chose to love or mourn or recoil from. The letters tell us whom and how he loved. He loved his sons. He loved John Berryman, John Cheever, Ralph Ellison, Martin Amis. He loved Alfred Kazin (whom he mostly disliked). He loved, to the end, Janis Bellow and their little daughter, Naomi Rose. He loved, even in death, Isaac Rosenfeld, the tumultuously inspired intimate of his youth (who nastily destroyed a hoard of his old friend's letters). He revered — but not always — thought, civilization, and what he named "the very image of man," all of which could be undone. He believed in outcry, and trusted the truth of his own. He was adept at witticism and outright laughter. He was serious in invoking whatever particle of eternity he meant by soul, that old, old inkling he was fearless in calling up from contemporary disgrace.

Like the novels and stories, the letters in their proliferation and spontaneity unveil the life — those sinews of it amenable to utterance — almost to its final breath. What happened soon afterward came to something less. On September 21, 2005, five months after Bellow's death, a celebratory symposium was convened at the 92nd Street Y in New York. The participants included British writers Ian McEwen, Martin Amis, and the critic

James Wood, the first two having flown from London for the occasion; William Kennedy and Jeffrey Eugenides completed the panel. Each spoke movingly in turn: joyfully reverential, heartfelt, intermittently (and charmingly) anecdotal, adoring — a density of love. There was mention of modernism, fictional digression, character, childhood, Chicago, crowded tenements, the immigrant poor. Riffing in homage, Amis delivered an imitation of Bellow's laugh, the delight and self-delight of it, the lifted chin, the head thrown back. But all this was a departure from the culminating sentiment — it *was* a sentiment, a susceptibility, a rapturous indulgence — that captivated and dominated these writerly temperaments. Wood: "I judge all modern prose by his. . . . The prose comes before and it comes afterward." Amis: "His sentences and his prose were a force of nature." McEwen: "The phrase or sentence has become part of our mental furniture. . . . Sentences like these are all you need to know about Saul Bellow." And so on. Understandable, plainly: superb novelists, stellar craftsmen, each one mesmerized by Bellow's unparalleled combinations.

Yet, despite these plenitudes, Saul Bellow was missing on that platform and in that auditorium teeming with admirers — as much missing there as, clothed in living flesh, he is an insistent presence in the letters. It was as if a committee of professional jewelers, loupes in place, had met to sift through heaps of gems strewn scattershot on a velvet scarf — the splendor and flash and glitter of opal and ruby and emerald, the word, the phrase, the sentence, the marvelous juxtapositions, the sublime clashes of style, the precious trove of verbal touchstones!

It was not enough. It was an abundant truth that diminished even as it aggrandized. A mammoth absence opened its jaws —

where was the century, the century that Bellow's reality-stung inquisitiveness traversed almost in its entirety, from Trotsky to Wilhelm Reich to Rudolf Steiner; where was the raw and raucously shifting society he knocked about in, undermined, reveled in, and sometimes reviled? Where was his imagined Africa, where were the philosophies he devoured, where were the evanescent infatuations he pursued, where was the clamor of history, and the defiant angers, and the burning lamentations for the beloved dead, the broken heart for Isaac Rosenfeld, whose writer's envy blazed, and for the father and brothers whose belittlements never left off hurting? And where, during that long tribute-laden afternoon in New York, was America itself?

Among the soon-to-be-forgotten novelists of our time, Saul Bellow stays on. Surely it is for the kaleidoscopic astonishments of his sentences that he lasts. But not only.

"Please, Stories Are Stories": Bernard Malamud

Hart and Schaffner are dead; Marx, ringed round with laurels, has notoriously retired. But the firm itself was dissolved long ago, and it was Saul Bellow who, with a sartorial quip, snipped the stitches that had sewn three acclaimed and determinedly distinct American writers into the same suit of clothes, with its single label: "Jewish writer." In Bellow's parody, Bellow, Malamud, and Roth were the literary equivalent of the much-advertised men's wear company—but lighthearted as it was, the joke cut two ways: it was a declaration of imagination's independence of collective tailoring, and it laughingly struck out at the disgruntlement of those who, having themselves applied the label in pique, felt displaced by it.

Who were these upstarts, these "pushy intruders" (as Gore Vidal had it), who were ravishing readers and seizing public space? Surveying American publishing, Truman Capote railed that "the Jewish mafia has systematically frozen [Gentiles] out of the literary scene." In a 1968 essay, "On Not Being a Jew,"

Edward Hoagland complained that he was "being told in print and sometimes in person that I and my heritage lacked vitality ... because I could find no ancestor who had hawked copper pots in a Polish shtetl." Katherine Anne Porter, describing herself as "in the direct, legitimate line" of the English language, accused Jewish writers of "trying to destroy it and all other living things they touch." More benignly, John Updike invented Bech, his own Jewish novelist, and joined what he appeared to regard as the dominant competition.

Yet it was not so much in response to these dubious preconceptions as it was to a rooted sense of their capacious American literary inheritance that all three unwillingly linked novelists were reluctant to be defined by the term "Jewish writer." "I am not a Jewish writer, I am a writer who is a Jew," Philip Roth announced in Jerusalem in 1963. And Bellow, pugnaciously in a 1988 lecture: "If the WASP aristocrats wanted to think of me as a Jewish poacher on their precious cultural estates then let them."

Bernard Malamud sorted out these contentious impulses far more circumspectly. "I am a writer," he said in an interview on his sixtieth birthday, "and a Jew, and I write for all men. A novelist has to, or he's built himself a cage. I write about Jews, when I write about Jews, because they set my imagination going. I know something about their history, the quality of their experience and belief. . . . The point I am making is that I was born in America and respond, in American life, to more than Jewish experience."

Though unexpressed, there lurks in all these concurring animadversions a fear of the stigma of the "parochial"—a charge never directed (and why not?) against Cather's prairie Bohemi-

ans, or the denizens of Updike's Brewer or Faulkner's Yoknapa-
tawpha. Still, it is not through sober public rhetoric but in the
wilder precincts of fiction that Malamud discloses his animating credo. It emerges in the clear voice of Levitansky, the an-
tihero of "Man in the Drawer," a harried Soviet-Jewish writer
whose work is barred from publication because it speaks human truths inimical to Stalinist policy. The American journalist who has worriedly befriended Levitansky asks whether he
has submitted any Jewish stories, to which the writer retorts:
"Please, stories are stories, they have not nationality.... When
I write about Jews comes out stories, so I write about Jews." It
is this unanchored drive to create tales, Malamud implies, that
generates subject matter — the very opposite of Henry James's
reliance on the story's "germ," the purloinings and devisings of
the observed world. "Stories are stories" is Malamud's ticket
to untrammeled writerly freedom. Except to Scheherazade, he
owes no social debts.

Despite this purist manifesto, Malamud is in fact steeped everywhere in social debt; his aesthetic is instinct with the muted
pulse of what used to be called moral seriousness, a notion gone
out of fashion in American writing, where too often flippancy
is mistaken for irony. Malamud, a virtuoso of darkest irony, refuses the easy conventions of cynicism and its dry detachment.
His stories know suffering, loneliness, lust, confinement, defeat;
and even when they are lighter, they tremble with subterranean
fragility. Older readers who were familiar with the novels and
stories in the years of their earliest publication will recall the
wonderment they aroused, beginning with the fables of *The
Magic Barrel,* as each new tale disrupted every prevailing lit-

erary expectation. The voice was unlike any other, haunted by whispers of Hawthorne, Babel, Isak Dinesen, even Poe, and at the same time uniquely possessed: a fingerprint of fire and ash. It was as if Malamud were at work in a secret laboratory of language, smelting a new poetics that infused the inflections of one tongue into the music of another. His landscapes, nature's and the mind's, are inimitable; the Malamudian sensibility, its wounded openness to large feeling, has had no successors.

When the ambient culture changes, having moved toward the brittleness of wisecrack and indifference, and the living writer is no longer present, it can happen that a veil of forgetfulness falls over the work. And then comes a literary crisis: the recognition that a matchless civilizational note has been muffled. A new generation, mostly unacquainted with the risks of uncompromising and hard-edged compassion, deserves Malamud even more than the one that made up his contemporary readership. The idea of a writer who is intent on judging the world—hotly but quietly, and aslant, and through the subversions of tragic paradox—is nowadays generally absent: who is daring enough not to be cold-eyed? For Malamud, trivia has no standing as trivial, everything counts, everything is at stake— as in "The Jewbird," where a bossy crow-like intruder named Schwartz invades a family, refuses birdseed in favor of herring, and to ingratiate himself tutors the dull son. But the father, sensing a rival for domination, is enraged, and this fanciful comedy ends in primal terror and murder. Pity leaves its signature even in farce.

"The Jewbird" is one of thirty-six stories in the Library of America's definitive three-volume publication (the third is

forthcoming) honoring Malamud's work on the hundredth an-
niversary of his birth; six of these Malamud himself never saw in
print. Also included in the pair of volumes are five novels: *The
Natural, The Assistant, A New Life, The Fixer,* and *Pictures of
Fidelman.*

A New Life may be the most overlooked of Malamud's long
fictions, perhaps because it has been mistaken for yet another
academic novel. But the sheath is not the sword, and *A New
Life* is as exquisite in its evocation of American transformation
as Gatsby himself. Reversing the classic theme of the young-
man-from-the-provinces, S. Levin, incipient wife stealer, "for-
merly a drunkard," is a refugee from the New York tenements
who leaves behind the grit of urban roil to be absorbed by village ways. Cascadia, the unprepossessing northwestern college
he joins as a low-ranking teacher, turns out to be precisely that:
a provincial village of the kind we might read of in an English
novel of rural life, with its petty hierarchies and spites and rival-
ries. Yet the local terrain — trees, flowers, green hills, pristine
vistas — is intoxicating to the city dweller, and here Malamud,
whose impoverished outer-borough warrens are uniformly
grim, writes peerlessly, as nowhere else, of proliferating natural
beauty. And in the vein of Huck Finn, who chooses damnation
over the lies of conventional morality, he casts a redemptive ra-
diance on the fraught flight of an adulterous woman and her for-
nicating lover. In its tormented, satiric, and startling undermin-
ings, *A New Life* — which, like *The Natural,* stands tonally apart
from Malamud's other work — is one of those rare transfiguring
American novels that turn wishing into destiny.

The Assistant and *The Fixer* are closer to the stories in their melancholy texture and feverish desperation. And as in the stories, a man's labor becomes his identity. Morris Bober tends a precarious grocery store, where his assistant hungers after love. The fixer, Yakov Bok, a worker in a brickyard, is unjustly imprisoned, walled in by an anti-Semitic blood-libel charge. Each person's fate pursues him: Fidelman in Rome, "a self-confessed failure as a painter," is stalked by the elusive Susskind, who covets Fidelman's suit. Leo Finkle, a rabbinical student, is hounded by Salzman the marriage broker. Alexander Levine, "a black Jew and an angel to boot," appears to Manischevitz, a tailor mired in suffering. Rosa, a maid in thrall to her lover, wheedles a pair of shoes out of the dignified professor whose rooms she cleans. Apparitions, stalkings, houndings, claims and demands: unbidden, duties and obligations fall on Malamud's characters with the power of commandments. The pursuer and the quarry are each other's double; through self-recognition, repugnance is conjured into acquiescence. In the shifting kaleidoscope of all these whirling tales, Malamud's quest is for renewal — freedom from the shackled self. Some have argued, not unpersuasively, that his humble Jews are stand-ins for universal suffering: in fiction as in life, living human beings ought not to be thrust into the annihilating perils of metaphor. Malamud easily escapes these transgressive erasures — the allegorical Jew, the Jew-as-symbol — through the blunt and earthy specificity of his ordinary Jews: census taker, shoemaker, bookseller, night school student, baker, egg candler, peddler, janitor, tailor (several), grocer (several, failing), taxi driver, actor, painter (failed), writer (several, failed). Wrenched into life by a master fabulist, they breathe, feel, yearn, struggle.

Then with all these believable Jews on hand, is Malamud a "parochial" writer, after all? Yes, blessedly so, as every sovereign imaginative artist is obliged to be, from Dickens to Nabokov to Flannery O'Connor to Malamud himself: each one the sole heir to a singular kingdom.

W. H. Auden at the 92nd Street Y

There must be sorrow if there can be love.
—from "Canzone"

Ah, the fabled Sixties and Seventies! Jack Kerouac and William Burroughs! The glorious advent of Howling! Of Getting Stoned! The proliferation of Ginsbergian Exclamation Points!

To secure the status of their literary subversion, these revolutionary decades were obliged, like the cadres of every insurrection, to denigrate and despise, and sometimes to blow up, their immediate predecessor, the Fifties — the middling middle, the very navel, of the twentieth century. The Fifties, after all, were the Eisenhower years, stiff and small like Mamie's bangs (and just as dated), dully mediocre, constrained, consumerist, car-finned, conformist, forgettable, and stale as modernism itself. Randall Jarrell, one of its leading poets and critics, named this midcentury epoch "the Age of Criticism" — and what, however he intended it, could suggest prosiness more? And what is prosiness if not the negation of the lively, the living, the lasting, the daring, the true and the new?

The reality was sublimely opposite. It was, in fact, the Age of Poetry, a pinnacle and an exaltation; there has not been another since. Its poets were more than luminaries—they were colossi, their very names were talismans, and they rose before us under a halo of brilliant lights like figures in a shrine. It *was* a kind of shrine: the grand oaken hall, the distant stage and its hallowed lectern, the enchanted voices with their variegated intonations, the rapt listeners scarcely breathing, the storied walls themselves in trance—this was the Poetry Center of the 92nd Street Y in the heart of the twentieth century.

And bliss was it to be young and enraptured in the dusk of that cavernous arena, at $20 per season ticket! It was the Age of Poetry precisely because it was still the age of form, when form, even when abandoned, was there to *be* abandoned. (Wild child Allen Ginsberg knew and revered his progenitors, even as he tossed them to the winds.) And form, in those disparaged Fifties, meant difficulty in the doing; meant the hard practice of virtuosity; meant the plumbing of language for all its metamorphoses and undiscovered metrics; meant the heritage of knowledge; meant, in order to aspire to limitlessness, the pressure of limits—rhyme, even rhyme, a thing of wit and brio, never an archaism. Poetry then had not yet fallen into its present slough of trivia and loss of encompassment, the herding of random images of minuscule perspective leading to a pipsqueak epiphany, a delirium of incoherence delivered, monotone upon monotone, in the cacophony of a slam.

Instead, a procession of giants. Their names are lasting, their lines permanent, and their voices (fortunately) recorded—

voices idiosyncratic, distinct, and so luxuriant in their unlikeness that it is an astonishment to see so many so large all alive at once. They have nothing in common but their dazzling mastery. And behold, on this selfsame platform, T. S. Eliot—a sacerdotal figure, the era's reigning literary pope, fake-Brit sonorities reverberating like a cathedral organ, grim and tragic, and as funereal as a marble tomb. And then W. H. Auden, capaciously contrapuntal, though they lived in consonance, Eliot born in 1888, Auden in 1907, Eliot an American who chose England, Auden an Englishman turned American. They died eight years apart, and knew the same world, the same political dooms, and the same return to the metaphysics of Christianity. On that broad stage Auden seemed at the time a lesser god: only Eliot could fill, as he once did, a football stadium. The public Eliot was a venerated monument that loomed unforgivingly, while Auden, even in public, had an air of plainness. Auden's reading was *spoken;* it had almost a casualness, a flatness, a matter-of-factness. He read poetry as if he were reading prose. He refused the vatic and the flamboyant. "I must try to eliminate from my own poetry false emotion, inflated rhetoric, empty sonorities," he once wrote. And in an interview: "Poetry is not self-expression." Eliot's thundering fame has since shrunk to a period datum, or, as in *The Four Quartets,* a mystical haze. But Auden, the most copious poet in English of the last century, unequaled for variety and scope—drama, lyric, ballad, sonnet, libretto, villanelle, and more—is the touchstone for all serious poets writing now.

And more: he is the necessary antithesis of Eliot: how clearly, two or three generations on, we can feel this! When the Twin Towers were felled by jihadist terror, and the world of Ameri-

can self-confidence ended not with a whimper but with a civ-
ilization-shattering bang, it was not "The Waste Land" that
was invoked to toll the bell of mourning. Not "London Bridge
is falling down falling down falling down ... *shantih shantih
shantih,*" that melancholic jigsaw of allusions, but the hard
mundane despairing concrete *presentness* of Auden's "September 1, 1939":

> *I sit in one of the dives*
> *On Fifty-second Street*
> *Uncertain and afraid*
> *As the clever hopes expire*
> *Of a low dishonest decade:*
> *Waves of anger and fear*
> *Circulate over the bright*
> *And darkened lands of the earth,*
> *Obsessing our private lives;*
> *The unmentionable odor of death*
> *Offends the September night.*

Here there are no symbols, no arcane "objective correlative."
Invasion and war, violence and dread, horizon and olfactory
nerve, place and time — the kernel of the hour, its history and
politics — are intimately knotted in these plainspoken lines,
open and direct and quick with fury. And never portentous in
the way of a shrouded haruspex.

Elsewhere, Auden's dry satiric voice can seize boisterously
and shamelessly on the vernacular, capsizing the lyrical with a
trickster's parodic quip:

Goddess of bossy underlings, Normality!
What murders are committed in thy name!
Totalitarian is thy state Reality,
   Reeking of antiseptics and the shame
   Of faces that all look and feel the same.
Thy Muse is one unknown to classic histories,
The topping figure of the hockey mistress.

(From "Letter to Lord Byron")

Though it may require a British staccato to rhyme "mistress" with "histories," the syncopated excitement of such a mélange of constructs, balanced by modulating couplets and quatrains, is Auden's signature; or call it the audaciously conflicting cadences of his breathing. His politics is metaphysics, his metaphysics is history, his history is humanity adrift in a labyrinth of its own making. In his heroic abundance he will catch hold of any form — or invent a new one — to assess, judge, condemn, praise, ruminate, fulminate, love; and once, in the name of literature, forgive:

Time that is intolerant
Of the brave and innocent,
And indifferent in a week
To a beautiful physique,

Worships language and forgives
Everyone by whom it lives;
Pardons cowardice, conceit,
Lays its honours at their feet.

Time that with this strange excuse
Pardoned Kipling and his views,
And will pardon Paul Claudel,
Pardons him for writing well.

(From "In Memory of W. B. Yeats")

No thought or feeling or concept eludes Auden: death, dream, doubt, loss, beauty, sex, love, fear, appetite, flight, wrath, hope, yearning, refuge, bliss, catastrophe, homage, savagery, pity, heritage, exile, nightmare — every motion, motive, and emotion of the range and plethora of human endurance. In one of his most impassioned elegies, addressed in supplication to the spirit of Henry James — "O stern proconsul of intractable provinces, / O poet of the difficult, dear addicted artist" — he contemplates the flooding in of all that the world contains or intimates, its "hinted significant forms":

As I stand awake on our solar fabric,
That primary machine, the earth, which gendarmes, banks,
    And aspirin pre-suppose,
On which the clumsy and sad may all sit down, and any who will
Say their a-ha to the beautiful, the common locus
    Of the master and the rose.

Our theatre, scaffold, and erotic city
And all the infirm species and partners in the act
    Of encroachment bodies crave
Though solitude in death is de rigueur for their flesh
And the self-denying hermit flies as it approaches
    Like the carnivore to a cave.

That its plural numbers may unite in meaning,
Its vulgar tongues unravel the knotted mass
　　Of the improperly conjunct,
Open my eyes to all its hinted significant forms,
Sharpen my ears to detect amid its brilliant uproar
　　The low thud of the defunct.

　　. . .

All will be judged. Master of nuance and scruple,
Pray for me and for all writers living and dead;
　　Because there are many whose works
Are in better taste than their lives; because there is no end
To the vanity of our calling; make intercession
　　For the treason of all clerks.

These are verses that can be understood, beyond the literary invocation that is their conceit, as philosophical advocacy, or even as a kind of crooked incantation, forsaking easy eloquence. They decline to chant or sing, and never has rhyme been so inconspicuous, while at the same time insinuating its sly and stealthy beat. Auden is a poet—no, *the* poet—of unembarrassed intellect. Ideas are his emotions, emotions are his ideas. His successors and inheritors can be named in an uncommonly short list—contemporary poets for whom the lyrical ear and the all-seeing eye and the mind in fever are entwined with the breath and bread of the world; and to whom history, that multitudinous ghost, is no stranger.

Perhaps there is no extant recording of Auden reading "At the Grave of Henry James" on the august stage of the 92nd Street Y half a century ago. Or perhaps there is. Still, whatever it was that we anointed listeners were once blessed to hear, the timbre and the rasp, and the Hurrah and the Alas, of the poet's voice can be found again in these plain lines:

> ... *Only the past*
> *Is present, no one about but the dead as,*
> *Equipped with a few inherited odds and ends,*
>   *One after another we are*
> *Fired into life to seek the unseen target where all*
> *Our equivocal judgments are judged and resolved in*
>   *One whole Alas or Hurrah.*

Fanatics

MILENA JESENSKÁ, KAFKA'S TRANSLATOR AND lover, has left us a useful and persuasive definition of fanaticism: "that absolute, unalterable necessity for perfection, purity, and truth." It was Kafka she meant.

Then let us now praise fanaticism, how it binds the like and the unlike, how it aspires to purity, how it engenders art at its most sublime, seeking the visionary and the inescapable; and how it reveres the ascendancy of its desires.

Kafka, a fanatic of language, was not alone. America had its own language fanatics, of which he was unaware. In the novel we know as *Amerika* (*The Man Who Disappeared*, also called *The Stoker*), anomalous characters populating his American scenes are rife; but Kafka's imagination, capaciously strange though it was, could not have conceived of the American Hebraists, as prodigiously single-minded as himself, who were thriving in the very years he was at work on *Amerika*.

That Kafka contended with his native German even as he powerfully embraced it is one of the salient keys to his character: the key is in hand, but there is no lock for it to fit into. German was his, ineradicably, yet insecurely. His famously self-lacerating lament — that Jews who wrote in German had "their hind legs stuck in parental Judaism while their forelegs found no purchase on new ground" — suggests some small helpless underground animal futilely attempting to escape its burrow. But when he crucially, even triumphantly, announced, "I am made of literature and nothing else," it could only mean that it was German idiom and essence, German root and rootedness, that had formed and possessed him.

Why, then — early in life until late, and with strenuous diligence — did he pursue the study of Hebrew? The notebooks that survive (archived in the National Library of Israel) are redolent of an ironic pathos: an earnest schoolboy's laboriously inked vocabulary lists, Hebrew into German, in the very hour that the world's most enduring masterworks were spilling from this selfsame pen. When at twenty-nine Kafka was first introduced to Felice Bauer, the young woman to whom he would be twice engaged but would never marry, he thought her unprepossessing, but was nevertheless instantly drawn to her talk: she was, she told him, studying Hebrew.

The American Hebraists, poets who in their youth had emigrated from Eastern Europe, were Kafka's contemporaries. They were also his peers in language fanaticism: they too were made of language and nothing else — but the language that formed and possessed them was Hebrew. Unlike Kafka's feverish wrestling with the fraught and unseemly question of hind legs and forelegs, they were consumed, body and soul, with no ambivalence of belonging, by Hebrew. Not only were they fanatics in their claim of intimately ingrained ownership of Hebrew, its godlike guardians and creators, they were fanatics in their relation to their new environment. English was all around them, awaiting their mastery; and they did become masters of English, and still it was Hebrew that inflamed them. Nor were they — unlike Kafka — torn by incessant doubt and self-repudiation. Scattered in cities all over America, they sat in tranquil rooms, on new ground, immersed in the renewing sublimity of the ancient alphabet.

And then they disappeared.

Kafka did not disappear.

No Hebraist poets inhabit his *Amerika,* but we can try to imagine, had he journeyed, like his protagonist Karl, to the real America, and encountered, say, Preil or Halkin or Regelson, would they recognize one another as equally eaten by that glorious but perilous worm, literary fanaticism?

Transcending the Kafkaesque

How, after all, does one dare, how can one presume? Franz Kafka, named for the fallen crown of a defunct empire, has himself metamorphosed into an empire of boundless discourse, an empire stretched out across a firmament of interpretation: myth, parable, allegory, clairvoyance, divination; theory upon thesis upon theophany; every conceivable incarnation of the sexual, the political, the psychological, the metaphysical. Another study of the life? Another particle in the deep void of a proliferating cosmos. How, then, does one dare to add so much as a single syllable, even in the secondary exhalation of a biography?

One dares because of the culprits. The culprits are two. One is "Kafkaesque," which buries the work. The other is "transcend," which buries the life. A scrupulous and capacious biography may own the power to drive away these belittlements, and Reiner Stach's mammoth three volumes (only the second and third have appeared in English so far) are superbly tempered for exorcism. With its echo of "grotesque," the ubiquitous term "Kafkaesque" has long been frozen into permanence, both in the dictionary and in the most commonplace vernacular. Comparative and allusive, it has by now escaped the body of work it is meant to evoke. To say that such and such a circumstance is Kafkaesque is to admit to the denigration of an imagination that has burned a hole in what we take to be modernism—even in what we take to be the ordinary fabric and intent of language. Nothing is "like" "The Hunger Artist." Nothing is "like" "The Metamorphosis." Whoever utters "Kafkaesque" has neither fathomed nor intuited nor felt the impress of Kafka's devisings. If there is one imperative that ought to accompany any biographical or critical approach, it is that Kafka is not to be mistaken for the Kafkaesque. The Kafkaesque is what Kafka presumably "stands for"—an unearned and usurping explication. And from the very start, serious criticism has been overrun by the Kafkaesque, the lock that portends the key: homoeroticism for one maven, the father-son entanglement for another, the theological uncanny for yet another. Or else it is the slippery commotion of time; or of messianism; or of Thanatos as deliverance. The Kafkaesque, finally, is reductiveness posing as revelation.

The persistence of "transcend" is still more troublesome. What is it that Kafka is said to transcend? Every actual and factual aspect of the life he lived, everything that formed and informed him, that drew or repelled him, the time and the place, the family and the apartment and the office—and Prague itself, with its two languages and three populations fixed at the margins of a ruling sovereignty sprawled across disparate and conflicting nationalities. Kafka's fictions, free grains of being, seem to float, untethered and self-contained, above the heavy explicitness of a recognizable society and culture. And so a new and risen Kafka is born, cleansed of origins, unchained from the tensions, many of them nasty, of Prague's roiling German-Czech-Jewish brew, its ambient anti-Semitism and its utopian Zionism, its Jewish clubs and its literary stewpot of Max Brod, Oskar Baum, Franz Werfel, Otto Pick, Felix Weltsch, Hugo Bergmann, Ernst Weiss. In this understanding, Kafka is detached not from the claims of specificity — what is more strikingly particularized than a Kafka tale? — but from a certain designated specificity.

In an otherwise seamless introduction to Kafka's *Collected Stories,* John Updike takes up the theme of transcendence with particular bluntness: "Kafka, however unmistakable the ethnic source of his 'liveliness' and alienation, avoided Jewish parochialism, and his allegories of pained awareness take upon themselves the entire European — that is to say, predominantly Christian — malaise." As evidence, he notes that the Samsas in "The Metamorphosis" make the sign of the cross. Nothing could be more wrong-headed than this parched Protestant misapprehension of Mitteleuropa's tormented Jewish psyche. (Danilo Kiš, Isaac Babel, Elias Canetti, Walter Benjamin, Gershom Scholem, Stefan Zweig, Josef Roth: from these wounded ghosts, a chorus of knowing laughter.) The idea of the parochial compels its opposite: what is not parochial must be universal. And if the parochial is deemed a low distraction from the preponderant social force — "that is to say, predominantly Christian" — then what is at work is no more than supercilious triumphalism. To belittle as parochial the cultural surround ("the ethnic source") that bred Kafka is to diminish and disfigure the man — to do to him what so many of Kafka's stories do to their hapless protagonists.

As biographer, Reiner Stach will have none of this. Nowhere

in *The Decisive Years* nor in *The Years of Insight* does he impose on Kafka an all-encompassing formula. He offers no key, no code, no single-minded interpretive precept: the Kafkaesque is mercifully missing. Instead, he allows Kafka's searing introspections, as they emerge from the letters and diaries, to serve as self-defining clues. Kafka saw his stories not as a reader or critic will, but *from the inside,* as the visceral sensations of *writing.* "I am made of literature; I am nothing else and cannot be anything else," he announced to Felice Bauer, the woman he would never marry. It was a statement meant not so much metaphorically as bodily. At twenty-nine, on September 23, 1912, he exulted in his diary as an exhausted but victorious long-distance swimmer, on completing a marathon, might:

> The story, "The Judgment," I wrote during the night of the 22nd, from 10 P.M. to 6 A.M., in one sitting. I could hardly pull my legs out from under the desk; they had become stiff from sitting. The frightful exertion and pleasure of experiencing how the story developed right in front of me, as though I were moving forward through a stretch of water. Several times during the night I lugged my own weight on my back. How everything can be hazarded, how for everything, even for the strangest idea, a great fire is ready in which it expires and rises up again. . . . At 2 A.M. I looked at the clock for the last time. As the maid came through the front room in the morning, I was writing the last sentence. Turning off the lamp, the light of day. The slight pains in my chest. The exhaustion that faded away in the middle of the night. . . . Only in this way can writing be done, only in a context like this, with a complete opening of body and soul.

Stach will go no further than Kafka's own reflections and admissions. In this restraint he follows Kafka himself: on no account, he instructed the publisher of "The Metamorphosis," should the insect be pictured. He saw explication as intrusion, and willful interpretation as a false carapace. A premonitory authorial warning: he was already warding off the Kafkaesque.

In refusing the critic's temptation, Stach is freed as biographer. Open to him is the limitless web of the societal, the political, the historical, the customary, the trivial; everything material, explicit, contemporaneous — sometimes day by day, on occasion even hour by hour; the trains and the telephones; the offices and the office machines; the bureaucrats and their litigations; the apartment and the family's noises. In brief: the parochial, in all its dense particularity. The biographer excavates, he does not transcend, and through this robustly determined unearthing he rescues Kafka from the unearthliness of his repute.

Foremost is the question of language. In Prague, Czechs spoke Czech, Germans spoke German, Jews spoke German. Kafka's ruminations on his relation to the language he was born into are by now as familiar (or as overfamiliar) as his face in the photographs, and equally revealing of shrouded pain. Jews who wrote in German, he lamented, resembled trapped beasts, neither at home in their native idiom nor alien to it. They lived, moreover, with three impossibilities: "the impossibility of not writing, the impossibility of writing German, the impossibility of writing differently." To which he added a fourth, "the impossibility of writing."

Kafka's prose has been universally lauded as spare, somber, comic, lucent, almost platonically pure; but many of those who acclaim it are compelled to read through the art of the translator. Shelley Frisch, Stach's heroic American translator, movingly reproduces his intended breadth and pace and tone, though now and again she is tempted to transmute the biographer's turns of phrase into popular local catchwords ("tickled pink," "thrown for a loop," "let off steam," "went to temple," "right off the bat," and many more). This is not altogether a failing, since it is Stach, not Kafka, whom these displaced Americanisms represent; but at the same time they serve to remind us that the biographer, whose *Muttersprache* is German, comes to Kafka's idiom with the deep linguistic affinities that only a native German, one who is also a literary writer, can assert. It is with such felt authority that Stach looks back at Kafka's writing — not to say how and what it is, but rather how and what it is not: "There were no empty phrases, no semantic impurities, no weak metaphors — even when he lay in the sand and wrote postcards." Yet there is another side to Stach's closeness to Kafka's rhetoric. When Kafka declared the impossibility of writing German, it was plainly not the overriding mastery of his language that was in doubt, but its ownership — not that German did not belong to him, but that he did not belong to it. German was unassailably at the root of his tongue; might he claim it societally, nationally, as a natural inheritance, as an innate entitlement? The culture that touched him at all points had a prevailing Jewish coloration. Family traditions, however casually observed, were in the air he breathed, no matter how removed he was from their expression. His most intimate literary friendships consisted entirely of writers of similar background; at least two, Max Brod and Hugo Bergmann, were seriously committed to Zionism. He studied Hebrew, earnestly if fitfully, at various periods of his life, and he attended Martin Buber's lectures on Zionism at the meetings of Bar Kochba, the Association of Jewish University Students. Unlike the disdainful Jewish burghers of Prague, who had long ago shed what they dismissed as an inferior *zhargón*, he was drawn to a troupe of Yiddish-speaking players from Poland and their lively but somewhat makeshift theater. He was a warm proponent of the work of Berlin's Jewish Home, which looked after the welfare and education of impoverished young immigrants from Eastern Europe. He read Heinrich Graetz's massive *History of the Jews;* he read *Der Jude,* the monthly founded by Buber; he read *Die Jüdische Rundschau,* a Zionist weekly; he read *Selbstwahr,* yet another Zionist periodical, whose editor and all of its contributors he knew. He also read *Die Fackel,* Karl Kraus's scourging satiric journal.

If Kafka's profoundest conviction ("I am made of literature") kept its distance from these preoccupations and influences, he nevertheless felt their pressure in the way of an enveloping skin. His commanding conundrums, including the two opposing impossibilities—writing and not-writing—are almost suffocatingly knotted into Jewish insecurities. Zionism was one symptom of this powerful unease; and so was Kraus's repudiation of Zionism, and his furious advocacy of radically self-obscuring assimilation.

It is difficult to refrain from pondering how a biographer (and a biographer is inevitably also a historian) will confront these extremes of cultural tension. Every biography is, after all, a kind of autobiography: it reveals predispositions, parallels, hidden needs; or possibly an unacknowledged wish to take on the subject's persona, to become his secret sharer. The biographer's choice of subject is a confession of more than interest or attunement. The desire to live alongside another life, year by year, thought for thought, is what we mean by possession. And for Stach to be close, both as a given and as a fortuity, to Kafka's language can hardly reflect the full scope of his willed immersion. He must also come close to Jewish foreboding—a foreboding marinated in the political and tribal and linguistic complexities of Austria-Hungary at the turbulent crux of its demise. Much of Kafka's fiction—*The Trial, The Castle,* "In the Penal Colony"—has too often made of him a prognosticator, as if he could intuit, through some uncanny telescope, the depredations that were soon to blacken Europe in the middle of the twentieth century. But the times required no clairvoyance; Jewish disquiet was an immediacy. At fourteen, Kafka witnessed anti-Semitic rioting that had begun as an anti-German protest against the Habsburg government's denial of Czech language rights. At thirty-seven, three years before his death, and with *The Castle* still unwritten, he saw Prague's historic Altneu synagogue attacked and its Torah scrolls torched. "I've been spending every afternoon outside on the streets, wallowing in anti-Semitism," he recounted. "The other day I heard the Jews called *Prasivé plenemo* [mangy brood]. Isn't it natural to leave a place where one is so hated? . . . The heroism of staying on nevertheless is the heroism of cockroaches that cannot be exterminated even from the bathroom."

Post-Holocaust, all this must sting a susceptible German ear; note that Zyklon B, the genocidal gas of the extermination camps, was originally used as an insecticide. Yet there are reminders still more unsettling. Because a biography of Kafka will perforce include minor characters—his sisters Elli, Valli, and

Ottla, for instance — it must finally arrive at Kafka's afterlife, the destiny he did not live long enough to suffer: that zone of ultimate impossibility wherein all other impossibilities became one with the impossibility of staying alive. Between 1941 and 1943, all three sisters perished, Elli and Valli in Chelmno, Ottla in Auschwitz. They hover over Kafka's biographies — this one, and all the rest — like torn and damaged Fates. Stach is never unaware of these points of connection; at first, uninvited, *sotto voce*, behind the scenes, in quiet recognition, they pierce the weave of his narrative. But by the time he attains his coda, Stach's watchful voicing of the fraught history of the Jews of central Europe during the passage of Kafka's life will have risen to a thunder.

And while a biographer may be willy-nilly a historian, and subliminally an autobiographer, he is, even more so, a species of novelist — of the nineteenth-century, loose-baggy-monster variety. He is in pursuit of the whole trajectory of a life, beginning, middle, end: chronology is king, postmodern fragmentation unwelcome, landscapes lavish, rooms and furnishings the same, nothing goes unnoticed. The biographer is a simulacrum, say, of George Eliot, who places her characters against the background of a society rendered both minutely and expansively, attending to ancestry, religion, economic standing, farming, banking, business, reading, travel, and more. Stach, in this vein, is doubtless the first to give so plentiful an account of the activities of the Prague Workers' Accident Insurance Company, the government agency where Kafka was employed as a lawyer from 1908 until 1918, when advancing tuberculosis forced his retirement. That he divided his day into office and work — by declaring them antithetical — is itself a type of credo; but Kafka's exalted literary image has too readily obscured the press of the quotidian. What did Kafka *do,* what were his everyday responsibilities? Stach lifts the dry-as-dust veil:

> If an industrialist submitted an appeal, the office had to establish proof that the safety precautions of the firm in question were not up to the latest standards. But what were the latest standards? They could not be definitively stipulated with ordinances; they had to be continually reestablished, if possible by personal observation. Kafka, who already had legal expertise, quickly acquired the technical know-how; he attended courses and traveled through northern Bohemian industrial cities. Next to the swaying stacks of appeals on his huge office desk there was an array of journals on accident prevention . . . in the areas in which he specialized — particularly the woodworking industry and quarries.

And so on and so on. An annual report, ostensibly submitted by Kafka, is titled "Accident Prevention Rules for Wood Planing Machines," and recommends the use of a cylindrical spindle. It is accompanied by illustrations of mutilated hands. In the wake of World War I, with its tens of thousands of maimed and shell-shocked soldiers, he was to see far worse.

For Kafka, none of these lawyerly obligations, however demanding, counted as work. No matter that his acumen and skills were regularly rewarded with promotion by the pair of bookish and obliging men who were his superiors, and though he was deemed so valuable that they contrived to have him exempted from military service, he felt depleted, and even assaulted, by the very papers his own hand produced. Of this necessarily official language he wrote bitterly, "I am still holding all of it in my mouth with revulsion and a feeling of shame, as though it were raw flesh cut out of me (that is how much effort it cost me) . . . everything in me is ready for lyrical work, and a work of that kind would be a heavenly resolution and a real coming alive for me, while here, in the office, because of such a wretched document I have to tear from a body capable of such happiness a piece of its flesh." And again, with the emphasis of despair: *"real hell is there in the office; I no longer fear any other."* And yet another tightening of the vise: "For me it is a horrible double life from which there is probably no way out except insanity."

At two o'clock in the afternoon, at the close of the six tormenting hours in the office, he escaped to the family apartment, a noisy and crowded habitat that was less a refuge than a second entrapment. Seven persons occupied these cramped and untranquil rooms: the blustering bullying paterfamilias, the compliant mother, the three daughters, the discontented son yearning for privacy and quiet, and a live-in maid. Kafka's bedroom, the burning vortex of his nocturnal writing, lay between the parlor and his parents' room; it was a passageway for his father's comings and goings, early and late, trailing his bathrobe. And the apartment, like the office, had its own distinct raison d'être: it was the ground, the support, and the indispensable source of administrative personnel for the family shop, a successful fancy-goods emporium with numerous employees. Since both parents put in many hours there, and all family members were obliged to do the same, in this way the shop fed the apartment, and the apartment fed the shop. Hermann Kafka, the son of a *shochet* — a ritual butcher — had risen from a burdened childhood in a backward rural village to bourgeois respectability, and was impatient with any deviation from conventional expectations. Ottla, the youngest daughter, was attracted to the countryside and aspired to farming—a far cry from her duties in the shop. Franz was still another riddle. At the dinner table he confined himself to an ascetic diet of mainly fruits and nuts, masticating each mouthful thirty-two times, according to the nutritional tenets of Fletcherism. But his most controversial habit was sleeping in the afternoon after leaving the office: this was to secure a usable wakefulness for the sake of his work—his true work—in the apartment's welcome middle-of-the-night silence. Sleeping in the afternoon, during shop hours? To the business-minded father, this was incomprehensible; it was delinquent.

Kafka's delinquency became still more scandalous when he was recruited to take on the ownership and management of an asbestos factory, in partnership with the ambitious husband of his newly married sister Elli. Hermann Kafka approved of his son-in-law's entrepreneurial plans, but since family money was being dedicated to this enterprise, and the young man was an untried stranger, it was imperative that a blood relation contribute to the stability and probity of the business. At first Kafka attempted to fulfill a commitment he had never sought—the literature-besotted son as industrialist!—and grudgingly gave his afternoons to the factory, which meant sacrificing his nights. Despite his father's irritable proddings, he could not keep up even a pretense of interest (he was at this time far more absorbed in the precarious fortunes of the Yiddish players he had befriended), and at length the business failed. The record Kafka left of it is oblivious to product and profit-and-loss; and though

conceivably he might have appraised the factory and its perilously superannuated machines through the eyes of the workers'
accident official, it was instead the fevered midnight writer who
observed "the girls in their absolutely unbearably dirty and un-
tailored clothing, their hair unkempt, as though they had just
got out of bed, their facial expressions set by the incessant noise
of the transmission belts and by the separate machine that is au-
tomatic but unpredictable, stopping and starting. The girls," he
went on,

> are not people — you don't say hello to them, you don't apol-
> ogize for bumping into them; when you call them over to do
> something, they do it but go right back to the machine; with
> a nod of the head you show them what to do; they stand there
> in petticoats; they are at the mercy of the pettiest power. . . .
> When six o'clock comes, however, and they call it out to one
> another, they untie their kerchiefs from around their necks and
> hair, dust themselves off with a brush that is passed around the
> room and is demanded by the ones that are impatient, they pull
> their skirts over their heads and wash their hands as well as they
> can, they are women, after all; . . . you can no longer bump into
> them, stare at them, or ignore them; . . . and you do not know
> how to react when one of them holds your winter coat for you
> to put on.

The kerchiefs, the skirts, the brush, the washing, the coat:
Walter Benjamin, in his discriminating musings on Kafka, concludes that "the gesture remains the decisive thing." "Each gesture," he writes, "is an event — one might even say, a drama — in

itself." And it is the factory girl's simple act of helping with a coat that has the power to embarrass, perhaps even to shame, the owner.

This drama of the minutely mundane was what Kafka demanded of Felice Bauer; it was an inquisition of the humdrum, a third degree of her every movement and choice. He wanted a description of her blouse, her room, her reading, her sleeping; what her employment entailed; how she was occupied when at leisure (she liked to go dancing, she practiced gymnastics). He wanted to claim and envelop her altogether. He repeatedly asked for her photograph, and he repeatedly sent his own. When in their accelerating daily — sometimes hourly — correspondence she abandoned the formal *Sie* and addressed him familiarly as *Du*, he fell into a trance of happiness.

Felice, a distant relation of Max Brod's visiting from Berlin, was introduced to Kafka at the Brod family dinner table. It was, apart from Brod's parents, a meeting of young people. Felice was twenty-five, Max twenty-eight, Kafka twenty-nine. Stach announces this unwittingly portentous occasion with a trumpet blast: "The history of human events, like intellectual and literary history, highlights certain dates; these are engraved in the cultural formation of future generations. . . . The evening of August 13, 1912 . . . changed the face of German language literature, of world literature." These grand phrases might have been applied to the somewhat more modest purpose of Kafka's presence that night: he and Brod had planned to look over a collection of sketches that Brod had long been urging his reluctant friend to agree to publish. The final decision about the order of the pieces was consummated in a colloquy after dinner, and what was to become Kafka's earliest publication, *Meditation,* was at last ready to be sent off. From the point of view of Kafka's biographers, though, what changed the face of world literature was not this small book by a little-known writer too perfectionist to release his work without lacerating self-doubt; it was the face of Felice Bauer. If not for the blizzard of revelatory letters that swept over her, enraptured and entreating to begin with, and then dismissive and retreating, Kafka's ponderings and sufferings during five crucially introspective years would have remained a vacuum: cries unheard, crises unrecorded.

Hers was a wholly ordinary face. Kafka, sitting across from the young woman from Berlin, at first mistook her for the maid. "Bony empty face," he later wrote, looking back at his initial impression, "displaying its emptiness openly. A bare throat. Her blouse tossed on. . . . A nose almost broken. Blond, somewhat stiff, unappealing hair, and a strong chin." He did not note the two black moles that are prominent in one of her photos, though absent in others, or, in nearly all of these, the bad teeth masked by closed lips. He learned that she worked for Parlograph, a firm selling dictation machines, having risen from typist to managerial status, and often traveling to trade fairs as company representative. If her looks and dress failed to attract him, her independence, reflected in her conversation, did. That she frequently read through the night impressed him. When she mentioned that she was studying Hebrew, he was captivated, and before the evening was over, the two of them were planning a journey to Palestine together — after which Kafka did not set eyes on her again for the next seven months. When he began to write to her, it was as a smitten and instantly possessive lover.

The Felice of Kafka's tumultuous letters was an imagined — a wished-for — figure. The actual Felice was an intelligent, practical, reasonable, efficient, problem-solving, generous woman who very soon recognized that she had been singled out by an uncommon rapture stirred by an uncommon nature. She was more than willing to respond, but every accommodating attempt resulted in a setback. He complained that she was not open enough; yet according to the standards and constraints of the proper middle-class background that defined her, how could she be? Her father was living apart from his family, her unmarried sister was suddenly pregnant, her brother had to be shipped off to America to escape reckless money entanglements. When these secret shames were finally disclosed, they were scarcely what put off Kafka; her habit of silence would bring him a deeper dismay. He had sent her an inscribed copy of *Meditation,* and though he appealed to her, piteously, for a comment ("Dearest, look, I want to have the feeling that you turn to me with everything; nothing, not the slightest thing should be left unsaid"), she never replied. Perhaps she could not: what was she to make of writing so enigmatic? She went to the theater, she read Ibsen; still, what was she to make of, say, "Trees," a story, if that is what it was, of four perplexing sentences? How was she to fathom such a thing?

> For we are like tree trunks in the snow. In appearance they lie sleekly and a little push should be enough to set them rolling. No, it can't be done, but they are firmly wedded to the ground. But see, even that is only appearance.

His passionate explanation — "I am made of literature and nothing else" — led to misunderstanding. Pragmatist that she was, she counseled moderation. And worse yet: it led to what she took to be understanding — she had begun to sense in him "seeds of greatness." And with all the sympathetic warmth of wishing to please him, she stumbled into a critical misjudgment (she offered to be close to him while he wrote) and lost him altogether. His shock at this innocent proposal turned into vehement resentment, bordering even on revulsion, as if she were intending to fleece him of his survival as a writer; and shock, resentment, revulsion culminated in one of his most wrenchingly monastic images of artistic self-entombment:

> Once you wrote that you wanted to sit by my side as I write; just keep in mind that I cannot write like that (even so I cannot write much), but in that case I would not be able to write at all. Writing means revealing oneself to excess, the utmost candor and surrender, in which a person would feel he is losing himself in his interaction with other people and from which he will always shy away as long as he hasn't taken leave of his senses — because everyone wants to live as long as he is alive.... Anything that writing adopts from the surface of existence ... is nothing, and caves in on itself at the moment that a truer feeling rattles this upper ground. That is why one cannot be alone enough when one is writing; that is why it cannot be quiet enough around one; the night is not night enough.... I have often thought that the best kind of life for me would be to stay in the innermost room of an extended locked cellar with my writing materials and a lamp.... What I would write! From what depths I would draw it up!

Here he was assuring the woman who trusted she would soon become his wife that the prospect of her coming near would threaten his capacity to live, and that rather than have her sit beside him, he would prefer to be immured underground. This ruthless detachment continued through two painful official engagements (the later embroiling him in the off-putting ritual of choosing the marital furniture and the conjugal apartment), until he had depleted Felice down to the very lees of her usable sustenance.

In the vista of Kafka's life, Felice is a promontory, partly because she occupied so large a tract of it, but also because of a simple bibliographical datum: she kept his letters. (He did not preserve hers.) She kept them through her marriage, and through her emigration to America in 1936, when escape from Nazi Germany became imperative, until her unremarked death in 1960 in a New York suburb. Beyond — or below — the promontory are the foothills, lesser outcroppings that reflect the configuration of the greater. Or put it that the letters to Felice expose the template, the very genome, of Kafka's character as it has revealed itself to biographers, and to Stach in particular; and by now they are seen to be *literature* as much as the canonical work itself. They underlie a binding continuum: from the diaries to the letters to Felice to the letters to Milena Jesenská to the letters to Max Brod to the prodigious one-hundred-page letter to Kafka's father — and even to a single sketch, ink on paper, drawn by Kafka. A stark black stick figure, stick elbows bent, stick legs outstretched among stick legs of table and chair, all of it spider-like. The spider's body — a human head — rests on the table. It is an image of defeat, surrender, despair, submission.

Milena Jesenská came to Kafka as a translator; in every way she was what Felice was not. Her eyes were as pale as Felice's, but rounder, and her nose was round, and her chin, and her mouth. Felice was a conformist: the furniture must be heavy and ornate, signaling a settled and prosperous marriage. Milena was a rebel, and to earn money in a lean time she was not above carrying luggage for travelers in the Vienna train station. She was a nimble writer and an ardent if contrarian spirit: "a living fire," as Kafka described her to Brod. Her mother was long dead, and her father, an eminent professor of dentistry, recognizing her exceptional gifts, sent her to an elite high school for Czech girls, where the classics and modern languages were taught and the arts were encouraged and cultivated. She and a handful of likeminded classmates made it a habit to loiter in Prague's literary cafés, where she encountered Ernst Pollak, ten years her senior, whom she eventually married. From her father's standpoint it was an insurrectionist act that estranged him from his daughter. The professor was a Czech nationalist, hostile to Germans, and especially averse to their Prague subdivision, German-identified Jews. After futilely confining Milena in a mental institution for some months, he dispatched her and the social embarrassment of her Jewish husband to Vienna—where, in a period of serious postwar scarcity, food was even harder to come by than in Prague. Only yesterday the capital of an empire, Vienna was now a weakened and impoverished outlier, despite its lively literary scene. It turned out to be an uneasy match: Pollak was a persistent philanderer and a dissatisfied writer manqué, impressively voluble in bookish circles but stymied on the page. It was he who introduced Milena to Kafka's still sparse publications, which inspired her to render "The Stoker" into Czech— the story that was to become the opening chapter of *The Man Who Disappeared,* his abandoned early novel. Kafka was admiring and gratified ("I find there is constant powerful and decisive understanding," he told her), and their correspondence began, rapidly turning intimate: Kafka's second limitless outpouring of letters to a young woman who kindled his longings and embodied his subterranean desires.

But if Felice had been a fabricated muse, as unresponsively remote from his idée fixe as a muse ought not to be, Milena was no muse at all. She provoked and importuned him from a position of equality; she was perceptive and quick and blunt and forward. Almost instantly she startled him: "Are you a Jew?" And though he had rarely spoken to Felice of the disquieting Jewish consciousness that perpetually dogged him (a self-punishing sensitiveness he and Brod had in common), to Milena he unburdened himself with a suicidal bitterness that in one ferocious stroke reviled and mocked the choking anti-Semitism he knew too well:

> I could sooner reproach you for having much too high an opinion of the Jews (me included) . . . at times I'd like to stuff them all, as Jews (me included) into, say, the drawer of the laundry chest, wait, open the drawer a little to see if they've all suffocated, and if not, shut the drawer again, and keep doing this until the end.

She had to put up with this; yet she summoned him, and he came, and in the Vienna woods one afternoon they lived out an idyll, the two of them lying on the forest floor, he with his head on her half-exposed breast. Together they schemed how she might leave Pollak; in the end she could not. He was himself not free; he was at this time engaged to be married to Julie

Wohryzek, a young woman whom Hermann Kafka, threatening and berating, disapproved of as déclassé; unlike Felice, she was not suitably respectable. Her father was a penniless cobbler and the *shammes* of a synagogue — worse, she occasionally fell into a low Yiddish phrase, and still worse, she had a "loose" reputation. Kafka had met her at a boardinghouse passing for a tuberculosis sanitorium; like him, she was there to convalesce. When Milena swept in, he disposed of this inflamed but short-lived attachment as no better than a dalliance, to be blown away like a stray straw. A space, then, was cleared for Milena: a landscape wherein the intellectual could be joined to the erotic. She filled it with her certainties and uncertainties, her conviction too often erased by ambivalence. Kafka's uncertainties ran deeper, and his mode of retreat was well practiced: "We are living in misunderstandings; our questions are rendered worthless by our replies. Now we have to stop writing to one another and leave the future to the future." To Brod, Milena sent an epitaph to the marriage that both she and Kafka had evaded. "He always thinks that he himself is the guilty and weak one," she wrote. "And yet there is not another person in the world who has his colossal strength: that absolutely unalterable necessity for perfection, purity, and truth." Milena outlived Kafka by twenty years. In 1944, she was arrested for sheltering Jews and aiding their flight; she perished in Ravensbrück.

Despite three failed engagements, Kafka never married. Yet he was not without such confidential support; there were, in fact, three loyally solicitous persons who took on a wifely role: his sister Ottla, Max Brod, and, at the close of his life, Dora Diamant. Ottla and Kafka had, early on, an obstacle in common — Hermann Kafka and his resistance to their independence. The monstrous (in size and in force) *J'accuse* that the son addressed, though never delivered, to the father now stands as yet another canonical work. Ottla's more quiet eruption came through stubborn acts of autonomy; unlike Kafka, she left behind both the family apartment and her role in the family economy. Hermann Kafka might mock his Czech employees as "my paid enemies," but Ottla chose to marry a Czech. And when the domestic commotion became unsustainable for Kafka's work, she gave him the use of the little neighborhood hideaway she had privately acquired. When his tuberculosis began to advance, and he declined to be admitted to yet another sanitorium (there were many such recuperative sojourns), with wifely devotion she cared for him at the longed-for farm she finally secured in the remote village of Zürau, where Kafka felt uncommonly serene. "I live with Ottla in a good little marriage," he assured Brod.

Brod was Kafka's confidant and champion, first reader, and also first listener: despite reticence and self-denigration, Kafka relished reading his work to friends. It was Brod who pushed Kafka to publish, pursuing skeptical editors on his behalf. "I personally consider Kafka (along with Gerhart Hauptmann and Hamsun) the greatest living writer!" he exclaimed to Martin Buber. "What I wouldn't do to make him more active!" Brod was himself energetic on many fronts: he turned out novels, plays, polemics, political broadsides; he ran to meetings for this cause and that; he labored to bridge the divide between Germans and Czechs; he promoted Czech writers and composers; and with Kafka (though not so diligently) he studied Hebrew. The two friends traveled to Weimar to visit Goethe's house, where each drew a sketch of the house and garden, and Kafka was all at once infatuated with the caretaker's young daughter.

But increasingly, Kafka's excursions away from Prague were solitary journeys to health resorts and tuberculosis sanitoriums; and inexorably in step with these, Stach's later chapters hurtle through harrowing episodes of fever, relentless coughing, days forcibly spent in bed, and finally, when the disease spread to the larynx, the threat of suffocation. Brod, always Kafka's anxious guardian, pressed him from the first to see the proper specialist and undertake the proper treatment. Kafka himself was oddly unperturbed: he believed that a psychosomatic element was the cause, and that, as he wrote to Ottla, "there is undoubtedly justice in this illness." As his condition worsened, he was compelled to give up his position at the Workers' Accident Insurance Company—which, like much of postwar Europe, was undergoing a political transformation. Habsburg officialdom was now replaced by Czech officialdom, in Munich swastikas were flying, and in Prague the decibels of anti-Semitism rang shriller. Hermann Kafka, uneasy in the company of his paid enemies, closed up his shop.

In the summer of 1923, Kafka—already seriously beginning to fail—entered into what can only be called a marriage, even if it had no official sanction and may never have been sexually consummated. It was his most daring personal commitment, and the only one untroubled by vacillation or doubts. Dora Diamant was twenty-five years old, the daughter of a rigidly observant Polish Hasidic family loyal to the dynastic rebbe of Ger. Though Zionism was frowned on as dangerously secular, Dora found her way to the writings of Theodor Herzl, broke from the constrictions of her background, and settled in Berlin. Here she worked with the children of the Jewish Home, the very institution Kafka had been so moved by in the past (and had pressed hard for Felice to support as a volunteer). Berlin was in chaos, reeling under strikes, riots, food shortages, and massive inflation. Despite every predictable discomfort and gravely diminishing funds, it was into this maelstrom that Kafka came to join Dora for one of the most tranquil intervals of his life. Half earnestly, half fancifully, they spoke of a future in Palestine, where, to make ends meet, together they would open a little restaurant. But the fevers continued to accelerate, and while Dora nursed him with singular tenderness, it became clear, especially under pressure from the family in Prague, that he was in urgent need of professional care. Another sanitorium followed, and then a hospital specializing in diseases of the larynx, always with Dora hovering protectively near. By now Kafka's suffering had intensified: unable to speak, he communicated on slips of paper; unable to swallow food, he was facing actual starvation, even as he struggled over proofs of "The Hunger Artist." At the last he pleaded for a lethal dose of morphine, warning — Kafka's deliberate paradox of the final paroxysm — that to be deprived of his death would count as murder. With Tolstoyan power, Stach carries us through these sorrowful cadences; the reader is left grieving.

Ottla; Hermann Kafka; Felice; Milena; Dora. They are, ultimately, no more than arresting figures in a biography. When the book is shut, their life-shaping influences evaporate. Not so Max Brod. He became — and remains — a lasting force in Kafka's posthumous destiny. In disobeying his friend's firm request to destroy the existing body of his unpublished manuscripts and to prevent further dissemination of those already in print, Brod assured the survival of the work of an unparalleled literary master. Solely because of this proprietary betrayal, *The*

Trial, The Castle, and *Amerika* (Brod's title for *The Man Who Disappeared*) live on; had there been no Brod, there would be no Kafka as we now read him. (And had Brod not fled German-occupied Prague for Tel Aviv in 1939, there would today not be a substantial cache of still unvetted manuscripts preserved in an Israeli national archive. It is from this trove that Stach's yet-to-be-published final volume will be drawn.) Savior though he was, Brod also manipulated whatever came into his hands. He invented titles for what was left untitled. He organized loose chapters into a sequence of his own devising. Having taken on the role of Kafka's authentic representative, he argued for what he believed to be the authoritative interpretation of Kafka's inmost meanings.

Stach ventures no such defining conviction. Instead, he ruminates and speculates, not as a zealously theorizing critic, but as a devoted literary sympathizer who has probed as far as is feasible into the concealments of Kafka's psyche. Often he stops to admit that "we cannot know." In contemplating the work, he tentatively supposes and experientially exposes. He eschews the false empyrean, and will never look to transcend the ground that both moored and unmoored his subject. In this honest and honorable biography there is no trace of the Kafkaesque; but in it you may find a crystal granule of the Kafka that was.

Nobility Eclipsed

On December 17, 2007, on the storied stage of the Poetry Center of the 92nd Street Y in New York, the Hebrew language — its essence, its structure, its metaphysic — entered American discourse in so urgent a manner as to renew, if not to inflame, an ancient argument. The occasion was a public conversation between Marilynne Robinson and Robert Alter: a not uncommon match of novelist with literary scholar. In this instance, though, the scholar is an English Department anomaly: not only a master of the Anglo-American corpus, but a profoundly engaged Hebraist and Bible translator and expositor, whose newly published volume of Englished Psalms is the evening's subject. The novelist too is exceptional among her contemporaries — a writer of religious inclination, open to history and wit, yet not dogged by piety, if piety implies an unthinking mechanics of belief. Robinson may rightly be termed a Protestant novelist, in a way we might hesitate to characterize even the consciously Protestant Updike. Certainly it is impossible to conceive of any other American writer of fiction who could be drawn, as Robinson has been drawn, to an illuminating reconsideration of Calvinism.

Protestant and Jew, writer and translator: such a juxtaposition is already an argument. The expectation of one may not be the expectation of the other. The novelist's intuition for the sacred differs from the translator's interrogation of the sacred. And beyond this disparity stands the inveterate perplexity, for English speakers, of the seventeenth-century biblical sonorities of the King James Version: can they, should they, be cast out as superannuated? The question is not so much whether the KJV can be surpassed as whether it can be escaped. From that very platform where Robinson and Alter sit amiably contending, a procession of the great modernists of the twentieth century (among them Eliot and Auden and Marianne Moore and Dylan Thomas) once sent out their indelible voices — voices inexorably reflecting the pulsings and locutions that are the KJV's venerable legacy to poets. And not only to poets: everyone for whom English is a mother tongue is indebted to the idiom and cadences of the KJV. For Americans, they *are* the Bible, and the Bible, even now, remains a commanding thread in the American language.

It is that thread, or call it a bright ribbon of feeling, that animates Robinson as she confronts Alter's rendering of Psalm 30, marveling at its "sacred quality of being," and at the psalmist's "I, this amazing universal human singular who integrates experience and interprets it profoundly. Any translation," she concludes, "is always another testimony." Here the novelist invokes exaltation in phrases that are themselves exalting, as if dazzled by a vast inner light washing out both the visual and the tactile: hence "testimony," an ecstatic internal urge. But Alter responds with an illustration that hints at dissent. The KJV, he points out, has "I will extol thee, O Lord; for thou hast lifted me up," while for "lifted me up" Alter chooses, instead, "drawn me up." The Hebrew word *dolah,* he explains, refers to drawing water from a well; the image is of a bottomless crevasse in the earth, fearfully identified in a later verse as "the Pit." Rather than turning inward, the translator uncovers sacral presence in the concrete meaning of the Hebrew, so that the metaphor of the well instantly seizes on weight and depth and muscle. Which approach is truer, which more authentic?

This, then, is the marrow — the unacknowledged pit — of the argument. And it becomes explicit only moments afterward, in Robinson's beautiful recitation of Alter's translation of Psalm 8, followed by Alter's reading of the Hebrew original. The contrast in sound is so arresting that Robinson is asked to comment on it. She hesitates: it is clear that to American ears the Hebrew guttural is as uncongenial as it is unfamiliar. Diffidently, courteously, she responds, "I have no Hebrew." "Well, *I* have," says Alter.

And there it is, the awful cut exposed: the baleful question of birthright. The translator asserts his possession of the language of the Psalms; is this equal to a claim that he alone is their rightful heir? Perhaps yes; but also perhaps not. The novelist, meanwhile, has embraced and passionately internalized those selfsame verses, though in their English dress — then is she too not a genuine heir to their intimacies and majesties? Never mind that Alter, wryly qualifying, goes on to address the issue of vocal disparity: "And if anyone thinks," he points out, "that he is reproducing the sound of Hebrew in English, he is seriously deluded." A translator's gesture of humility — the two musical systems cannot be made to meet; it cannot be done. But this comes as an aside and a distraction. What continues to hang in the air is Alter's emphatic declaration of ownership.

Hebrew in America has a bemusing past. The Puritans, out of scriptural piety, once dreamed of establishing Hebrew as the national language. Harvard and Yale in their early years required the study of Hebrew together with Latin and Greek; Yale even now retains its Hebrew motto. Divinity school Hebrew may be diminished, but endures. And though the Hebrew Bible is embedded in the Old Testament, its native tongue is silenced. "We have no Hebrew," admits biblically faithful America. Then can Hebrew, however unheard, be said to be an integral American birthright? Was Alter, on that uneasy evening in New York, enacting a kind of triumphalism, or was he, instead, urging a deeper affinity? Deeper, because the well of Hebrew yields more than the transports of what we have come to call the "spiritual." Send down a bucket, and up comes a manifold history — the history of a particular people, but also the history of the language itself. An old, old tongue, the enduring vehicle of study and scholarship, public liturgy and private prayer, geographically displaced and dispersed but never abandoned, never fallen into irretrievable disuse, continually renewed, and at the last restored to the utilitarian and the commonplace. Hebrew as a contemporary language, especially for poetry, is no longer the language of the Bible; but neither is it not the language of the Bible. And despite translation's heroic bridging, despite its every effort to narrow the idiomatic divide by disclosing the true names of things (the word itself, not merely the halo of the word), we may never see an America steeped in Hebrew melodies.

Yet once, for a little time, we did.

There was a period, in the first half of the twentieth century, when America — the land, its literature, its varied inhabitants and their histories — was sung in the Hebrew alphabet. Long epic poems on American Indians, the California Gold Rush, the predicament and religious expression of blacks in the American South, the farms and villages and churchgoers of New England, the landscape of Maine — these were the Whitmanesque explorations and celebrations of a rapturous cenacle of Hebrew poets who flourished from before the First World War until the aftermath of the Second. But both "cenacle" and "flourished" must be severely qualified. Strewn as they were among a handful of cities — New York, Cleveland, Boston, Baltimore, Chicago — they rarely met as an established group; and if they flourished, it was in driven pursuit of an elitist art sequestered in nearly hermetic obscurity. They were more a fever and a flowering than a movement: they issued neither pronouncements nor provocations. They had no unified credo. What they had was Hebrew — Hebrew for its own sake, Hebrew as a burning bush in the brain. Apart from those sociohistoric narratives on purely American themes, they also wrote in a lyrical vein, or a metaphysical, or a romantic. Though modernism was accelerating all around them, and had taken root through European influences in the burgeoning Hebrew poetry of Palestine/Israel, the American Hebraists almost uniformly turned away from the staccato innovations of the modernists. They were, with one or two exceptions, classicists who repudiated make-it-new mani-festos as a type of reductive barbarism. Rather than pare the language down, or compress it through imagism and other pro-sodic maneuvers, they sought to plumb its inexhaustible deeps. And when their hour of conflagration ebbed, it was not only because their readers were destined to be few. Hebrew had re-turned to its natural home in a Hebrew-speaking polity; many of the poets followed.

Who, then, were these possessed and unheralded aristocrats, these priestly celebrants unencumbered by a congregation, these monarchs in want of a kingdom? If, in retrospect, they seem no more than a Diaspora chimera, the fault may be ours: we have no Hebrew. Even so, in a revelatory work of scholarly grandeur that is in itself a hymn to Hebrew, Alan Mintz, profes-sor of Hebrew literature at the Jewish Theological Seminary, has revivified both the period and the poets. The capacious vol-ume he calls *Sanctuary in the Wilderness* is history, biography, translation, criticism, and more — a "more" that is, after all, an evocation of regret. The regret is pervasive and tragic. Think not of some mute inglorious Milton, but of a living and achiev-ing Milton set down in a society of illiterates unable to decipher so much as *abc,* and unaware of either the poet's presence or his significance. Yet Mintz never condescends; with honorable dif-fidence, he repeatedly refers to this majestic study as merely in-troductory, an opening for others to come.

Here let me offer a far smaller opening into that long-ago reach for the sublime. From a shelf harboring a row of bilin-gual Yiddish and Hebrew dictionaries, I pluck out a curious little Hebrew book that has journeyed with me since child-hood. It is so old that its pages are brittle and browning at the margins. The brownish-gray cover announces title and provenance: *RIVON KATAN, A Little Quarterly of POETRY and THOUGHT, Volume I, Number 1. Issued by the Hebrew Poetry Society of America. Three Dollars Yearly. Spring, 5704 (1944). Editor: A. Regelson.* As for the table of contents, its preoccupations and aspirations are self-evident:

> Henry A. Wallace: The Century of the Common Man
>
> N. Touroff: Can a Nation Become Insane?
>
> S. Hillel: Leo Tolstoy
>
> Ben Hanagar: Walt Whitman's Native Island
>
> Elinor Wylie: Velasquez (Hebrew by G. Preil)
>
> A. Regelson: The Poetry of Ibn Gabirol
>
> A. Regelson: Saul Tchernichovsky
>
> Ilya Ehrenberg: Plant and Child

Henry Wallace, Elinor Wylie, and Ilya Ehrenberg, all declaiming in Hebrew! And the Hebrew Poetry Society of America? It may be that A. [Abraham] Regelson, all on his own, comprised president, secretary, translation committee, and possibly the entire membership. Striving publications of this kind proliferated, many of larger note and longer duration. Most appeared exclusively in Hebrew, bearing redolent names: *Haderor* ("The Swallow"), *Hatoren* ("The Mast"), *Miqlat* ("Refuge") — although *Hadoar* ("The Post"), despite its more mundane designation and wider circulation, was as amply literary as the others.

Like the editor of the *Little Quarterly,* the poets who filled these periodicals were, without exception, a part of the great flood of turn-of-the-twentieth-century Eastern European Jewish immigration. Arriving as children or adolescents or in their early twenties, they came with a traditional Hebrew grounding behind them and an American education before them; and since their foundational tongue was Yiddish, they soon were easily and fluently trilingual. But to describe them merely as trilingual is to obscure their mastery. Any one of these poets might have leaped, if he chose, into the vigorous roil of Yiddish belles lettres and its thriving American journals. Or, even more prominently, there was the possibility of aspiring to the canon of English-language poets — to stand, in that era, beside Edwin Arlington Robinson, Wallace Stevens, and Robinson Jeffers.

Instead, what the Hebraists chose was patrimony — patrimony in the sense of rootedness in a primordial continuum. Though Yiddish too reveres and incorporates the legacy of Hebrew, the Hebraists turned away from Yiddish; despite its evolving high culture and literary achievements, it had its origins in an everyday vernacular, and — in the tumult and bustle of American acculturation — concerned itself less with the empyrean than with the tangles of daily life. Nor could these linguistic patricians be tempted by the powerful elasticity and breadth of English, however swept away they might be by the great English and American poets. Whitman in particular quickly became a kind of model and mentor, as well as a portal to a visionary America. Influences and tutelary spirits abounded, sometimes surprisingly. A case in point: Regelson felt himself so seized and claimed by W. B. Yeats that he composed an "Irish" poem in homage to the friendship of Yeats and Gogarty: *Shney barburim v'nahar* ("Two Swans and a River"). To experience the dazzlements of Regelson's own Englishing of this extraordinary narrative ode is to recognize how the choice of Hebrew may have occasioned a genuine loss to American (and Irish) literature.

Nor was it, astonishingly, a gain to Israeli letters. It may be a natural irony of history — natural because inexorable — that the establishment of Israel as a modern Hebrew-speaking nation in possession of an acclaimed and robustly expanding literature should have shut out the American Hebraists. It was not only that they were considered marginal to the Hebrew center, and on that account excluded. Worse yet, their very existence was unknown. Mintz opens his study by citing the dumbfounded observations of Zalman Shazar, Israel's third president and a literary figure in his own right, when on his first visit to America in the 1930s he discovered, like some Columbus encountering an unsuspected tribe, a Hebrew-intoxicated band of ascetics:

> In their isolated nobility, they attached themselves only to the intangible and absolute in the national spirit. They had complete mastery over the Hebrew language as if they lived in the Land of Israel, and they were utterly unreconciled and even oblivious to the surroundings in which they actually lived. In their loneliness, there was the sadness of being the chosen few, and in their sadness there was a marked but unexpressed pride. Just as they were alienated from their surroundings, so were they also separated from each other. . . . Most of them were scattered among various cities, as if no single Jewish community in America could handle them as a group. They appeared like a phalanx of knights loyal to the Hebrew language whose pride forbade them both from admitting the least hint of their difficulties to a Jew from Palestine and from paying the least heed to the seductions of English. . . . In this conscious renunciation of popular attention there was something of the self-gratification that proud artists allow themselves, something of the feeling of superiority enjoyed by monks offering obeisance to a Hebrew

Princess and serving her with no expectation of reward either
in this world or in the world to come, either in the Diaspora or
in the Land of Israel.

The tone of this anthropological survey as seen from the confident center is sympathetic and pitying — and condescending.
What the visitor saw was achingly partial, and may have derived
from the early Zionist "negation of the Diaspora," which viewed
the continuing presence of Jewish communities elsewhere
as poignantly superfluous if not tragically mistaken. And unlike self-denying monks or quixotically deluded knights alienated from their surroundings, these striving newcomers seized
on whatever bounty America held out, its public high schools
and universities, its landscapes and lore, above all its freedom
of self-invention. (What could be more self-invented than, say, a
poet residing in Cleveland raptly composing scores of sonnets
in Hebrew?) Rejection of English as a literary vehicle did not
mean rejection of English as the fulcrum of advancement in the
professions. Many, if not most, were engaged in building secular cultural institutions, including teachers' colleges, for the rig-
orous study of Hebrew language and literature, though always
with a wall of separation between the communal and the transcendent. The poetry was to be kept immaculately apart from
the pedagogy, and if the American Hebraists could be defined
by a common motif, it might be by the idea of separation. As
scholars and intellectuals, they were perforce set apart from the
mass of immigrant Jews, whose cultural attitudes and aptitudes
they disdained.

Their recoil, and often their satire, was, curiously, not very
different from that of Henry James during his 1905 excursion

among the streets and cafés of the Lower East Side, where he observed "the hard glitter of Israel," and predicted, thanks to Jewish linguistic infiltration, the debasement of English. "It was in the light of letters," he wrote, "that is in the light of our language as literature has hitherto known it, that one stared at all this impudence of the agency of future ravage." He could not have imagined, as irony has since abundantly noted, that out of those cacophonous streets and cafés would one day arise an army of Jamesian critics and scholars, bringing not ravage but homage. In scorning what he called the New Jerusalem, James saw a fallen nation; assessing the same population, so did the Hebraists. But while James proved to be a poor seer, the poets in their pridefulness may have intuited the heartbreak and hurt to come: the immigrants' children who became esoteric theorists and interpreters of Henry James (and Emerson and Hawthorne and all the rest) were at the same time Hebrew illiterates. As for the poets themselves, they were a prodigious generational accident, a miracle of literary confluence: who could have foretold an eruption of Hebrew-generative genius on the American continent—which, having no offspring, then came to nothing?

For his ambitious overview of this remarkable period, Mintz has chosen twelve out of the Hebraist cohort to contemplate in the round: the life, the work, the influences on the work, and each poet's particularized interiority. The twelve are not meant to be taken as representative of the whole: among such fiercely individuated minds, there can be no "type." Eisig Silberschlag, a professor of Hebrew literature at the University of Texas and a classical scholar who translated Aristophanes into Hebrew, had little in common with Gabriel Preil, an outlier singled out for his forays into modernism—the sole American Hebraist to achieve popular recognition in Israel. Though both wrote short lyric verses, Silberschlag's mature outlook was formed in Europe, where, in the 1920s, he earned a doctorate from the University of Vienna with a thesis, Mintz tells us, "on the economic relations between England and Russia during the reign of Catherine II." Israel Efros, a specialist in medieval philosophy and translator of Shakespeare, was consistently associated with universities; he founded Baltimore Hebrew College and was eventually called to be president of Tel Aviv University. As an ordained rabbi, Efros was singular among the Hebraists. Most had left traditional piety behind, no longer observing the punctilios of Jewish practice—a worldliness that brought some to law and medicine, and others to journalism. Like the American poets who were their close contemporaries, Wallace Stevens in his insurance office and William Carlos Williams on his doctor's rounds, they sought useful livelihoods. Preil alone appeared to cultivate an Emily Dickinsonian isolation.

Mintz illuminates the poets' biographies, brief as they are, with the skill of a pointillist. But it is in his analysis of the poems themselves that he is most masterly. "Analysis" is Mintz's word; it is inadequate to the reader's experience of what he brings off. Each central section of this massive volume is devoted to the body of work of a single poet, and culminates in the close reading of a single poem. Each poem is presented first in Hebrew, followed by Mintz's lucid English translation. But even "close reading" fails to approximate what is achieved here. A modesty—a felt trustworthiness—inhabits these multiple renderings: the goal is honest replication without embroidery. There is no intent to rival the original musically or sensuously. Mintz means the poem to be understood both for its inwardness and for the air it breathes; his critical vocabulary has the discerning force of insight. Analysis defines. Insight conveys.

And beyond insight is sympathy — sympathy as praise, as homage, and also as the kind of immersion in a writer's reason-for-being that will deliver him over to us as the writer himself would wish to be delivered. This requires a rare critical confidence that is crucially linked to critical humility. And nowhere is the fusion of confidence and humility more acutely displayed than in an extended preamble titled "The Apotheosis of Hebrew," which purposefully follows Mintz's more generalized introduction. Here Mintz concentrates, as he does elsewhere, on one poem by one poet, but with a difference. The poet is Regelson, and the poem is *Haquqot otiyotayikh* ("Engraved Are Thy Letters"), an intricately crafted paean to the Hebrew language: metaphysical, erotic, hubristic, fanatical. It aspires to steal, in effect, the recondite procreative fire of the Creator of the Universe, if that universe is seen as coequal with Hebrew in its infinite mystical manifestations and its internal morphological permutations. Mintz sets it apart for scrutiny neither as linguistically representative of the American Hebraists nor as aspirationally typical. He intends it, rather, as a touchstone, or what he identifies as "a privileged hermeneutical key," "the secret spring of American Hebraism," "a passion that could not speak its name." In *Haquqot otiyotayikh* Mintz sees the "repressed religious-libidinal attachment" that underlies the whole of the American Hebraist enterprise. "Yet without predicating this motor of desire," he writes, "it would be difficult indeed to understand the pertinacity and profusion of American Hebrew poetry. Were it not for the existence of an extraordinary excep-

tion to the general lack of self-awareness on this score, it would be presumptuous to 'psychoanalyze' a cultural phenomenon."
Regelson is that exception:

> Regelson's hymn to Hebrew is a dazzling work that is unlike any other poem in the corpus of modern Hebrew literature. It is an extravagant ode to a language offered by a lover in thrall to the object of his desire, which is figured as a beautiful woman. It is a classic anatomy, a literary form that exhaustively inventories the categories and components of its subject. It is a theological treatise on the divinity of Hebrew that advances an argument for linguistic pantheism. Written at the great hinge of the twentieth century, it is a historiosophical work that uses Hebrew as a marker for both the murder of European Jewry and the struggle for Jewish statehood. It is a polemic about the course of the revival of Hebrew and an attack on the purported guardians of its purity. It is an apologia for the life of a poet who, at the time of the writing, was stranded far from Zion. Above all else, the poem is a performance of virtuosity that, in its maximalist poetics, seeks to conjure up and demonstrate the full plastic and arcane resources of the Hebrew language.... Its explanatory power is crucial for an understanding of the project of American Hebraism as a whole ... a way into the inner spiritual and psychological world of American Hebrew poetry.

Mintz's speculative thesis — that a driven though submerged and surrogate eros accounts for the Hebrew intoxications of these poets — may or may not be true. But rivalry, whether underground or overt, can also be a sustaining engine. Gabriel Preil's turn to styles of modernism: was it an innate expression or a competitive urge? An unwilled imprint of the Zeitgeist or a shrewdly opportunistic choice? It is tempting to ask why Preil, alone among the Hebraists, was drawn to join the great contemporary wave of imagism and symbolism, the solitary and alienated emblematic "I," the new formless forms. The winner of an undeclared contest, he remains the only American Hebraist to survive obscurity and to have attained a modicum of ongoing posthumous notice. Surrounded by a culture wherein modernism was supreme, the others, faithful to the idioms of transcendence and eschewing dissonance and brokenness, may, in such an atmosphere, have appeared to be archaists. Preil fit in, and was welcomed. It is rivalry that determines who shall be prince and who pauper.

Shimon Halkin was among the princes. His beginning was as favored as his years of consummation. Mintz describes him at the acme of his repute:

As the occupant of the chair of Hebrew Literature at the Hebrew University of Jerusalem during the 1950s and 1960s, Halkin taught virtually every important writer and critic in the young state until his death at the age of eighty-eight in 1987. The force of his presence compelled attention to the body of his own poetry and fiction in face of the fact that his own writing flouted almost all the norms of the new Israeli literature of the time. Where the younger poets ... sought to bring the language of poetry closer to everyday speech, Halkin wrote in a high register using extreme figuration and a rarefied lexicon. Where they prized simplicity and the brief lyric, he championed complexity and the ambitious long poem. Where they took for granted that modern man is living in a world after faith,

Halkin made the search for God a central preoccupation of his poetic endeavor.... Halkin's poetry was accorded respect as much for the august power of the verse itself as for the influential figure of the poet who wrote it.

But Halkin was long accustomed to acclaim. On his arrival in New York at fifteen, he was already known to be prodigious in Hebrew, a reputation that accelerated even as Tennyson and Browning continued to stir him. His earliest poems were published in prestigious Hebrew journals during his high school years, and soon after college he was offered a stipend for literary translation and, more significantly, for the freedom to concentrate on his poetry. Still later, he won a competition for yet another stipend, this one awarded by Salman Schocken, the publisher of Kafka. He was financially liberated from the start.

He also won a more intimate competition. At William Morris High School in the Bronx he met the young Regelson, a boy three years his senior, who turned out, astonishingly, to be his double: a secret sharer of the elixir of Hebrew. Regelson too had been a prodigy: as a child in the *cheder*, the rabbi's schoolroom, he had composed, in fluent Hebrew, an interpretive synopsis of the thought of Rashi, the great medieval biblical annotator. At Morris High, the two teens conversed in Hebrew, and fell into passionate discussions of poetry and philosophy. Both were steeped in the English Romantics, and each early on knew himself destined for poetry: it was an idyll of elective affinities. Where they were most alike was in the style of their mature work, in what Mintz characterizes as "cascading sheets of electrifying figurative writing," and in the metaphysical/mystical/lyrical cast of their abiding inspirations. Their lives ran parallel in other ways. Both experienced interrupted sojourns in 1930s Palestine before settling there after the formal establishment of the Jewish state. Like Halkin, Regelson translated widely: Shakespeare, Milton, Herrick, Blake, Browning, Whitman, countless canonical others. Halkin, meanwhile, had already conveyed into Hebrew *The Merchant of Venice* and the whole of Whitman's *Leaves of Grass*. In 1975 Halkin was awarded the Israel Prize for literature. In 1972 Regelson was the recipient of the Chaim Nachman Bialik Prize, given in the name of the most illustrious Hebrew poet of the age.

In the end—rather, toward the middle—the parallels dissolved, the idyll cracked. The first telltale fissure began in boyhood, and came in the guise of an act of magnanimity, indeed an act of youthful noblesse oblige. As Halkin recounted it in a late memoir, he had received a letter from Regelson, written in an elegantly elevated Hebrew, and sent it on to his editor, the publisher of *Miqlat*, where Halkin's verses were already appearing. Impressed, the editor solicited and brought into print Regelson's first published poem. The younger poet had favored the older; but in becoming, through superior influence, Regelson's patron, he had also bested him.

And what had begun as affinity disintegrated further when the two young men entered City College of New York together. After a year, Regelson dropped out for reasons that remain unrecorded, though he was soon married and sooner yet the father of a son, the first of five children. Halkin went on to advanced degrees and a princely career as a revered professor of literature, while Regelson became, quite literally, a pauper who struggled to live by his pen, hoping to feed his children by the force of his imagination. But here Mintz, identifying Halkin's magisterial role as "a kind of tribune" in the republic of Hebrew letters, takes quizzical note of a problematic omission. Halkin was unstinting in "maintaining relations in person or by letter with writers scattered across several generations and writing about their work out of a sense of responsibility to the larger endeavor. . . . To the best of my knowledge," Mintz adds, "the only real notice that this prolific critic gave to Regelson and his body of work" was that single passing mention in Halkin's memoir of his own boyhood benevolence.

A bitter falling out, then. What happened?

Before I supply the answer (Mintz leaves the puzzle unresolved), I am obliged to confess that if I have returned to Regelson time and again, while scanting others among this study's glittering twelve, it is out of seeming partiality: Abraham Regelson was my uncle, my mother's brother. I hope before long to show that this apparent predisposition is made of nothing more substantial than air; yet consanguinity's advantage is ready access to buried knowledge — or call it comic melodrama, or the self-preening misadventures of a pair of contenders. According to Regelson's daughter, who serves as her father's archivist, the break erupted out of a volcanic charge of literary theft: Halkin accusing Regelson of plagiarism, Regelson accusing Halkin of plagiarism, each again the double of the other. Mutual recrimination, smoldering, became mutual contempt. Still, hidden in rivalry is its symbiotic secret: all competitiveness grows out of ferocious affinity.

This star-crossed operetta, however, has no satisfactory coda, and what, after all, is there to choose between Halkin and Regelson? Despite the serpent's tooth of disrespect, both were enmeshed in the great ancestral Judaic chain of word and idea.

Halkin held the scepter of influence, while the often impoverished Regelson toiled in journalism for bread — but who today
in America, beyond a minuscule handful of specialists (two,
perhaps three?) reads the American Hebraists? What does it
matter if a spangled recognition enthroned Halkin, or that Regelson knew himself to be self-made in the Hebrew image of
William Blake? Neither weighs in an America given to erasure
of a noble literary passage it has no tongue to name.

Then who is to blame? We are: *we have no Hebrew*. But who,
or what, really, is this culpable "we"? An admission: inescapably, the educated American mentality, insofar as it desires to
further self-understanding — and the educated American-Jew-
ish mentality even more so. The Hebrew Bible has long been
the world's possession, and those who come to it by any means,
through whatever language, are equals in ownership, and may
not be denied the intimacy of their spiritual claim. Yet spirit is
that numinous essence that flies above history, inhabiting the
moment's exquisite experience: it is common to all peoples,
hence native to none. History, in contrast, is linked to heritage,
and heritage — preeminently its expression in language — is
what most particularly defines a civilization. So when Alter re-
sponded to Robinson's reticent "I have no Hebrew" with his
quickly assertive "Well, *I* have," it was certainly as a translator
in confident command of superior skills — but not only. It was
also, irresistibly, a cry of kinship, and, even more powerfully, an
appeal to deep memory. Implicit in Alter's signal "have" is the
condition of the have-nots: an absence of even minimal Hebrew
literacy in a population unique among the nations of the West in
the authenticity of its biblical attachment.

Then who killed Hebrew in America?

I did, with my little bit of Hebrew, so little as to be equivalent to none. I knew Abraham Regelson as the affectionate uncle who gave me a 1910 British edition of Kipling's *Just So Stories* (with a gilt elephant and an Indian swastika on the cover); and I recall a postcard sent from 1930s Tel Aviv: a picture of a white building with an X marked over one window. "Here lives Bialik," my uncle wrote to his very young niece (who was innocent of the wonder of it). "And did you once see Shelley plain?" asks Edna St. Vincent Millay. I did not truly see my uncle plain until now, long after his death, when Mintz brought home to me "the poet's virtuosity: his encyclopedic mastery of the historical lexicon of the Hebrew language, his erudition in classical sources, and, most of all, his ability to take the language not just as given but to invent and proliferate provocative new words and dazzling constructions." Seductive gates these, through which I may not pass, forbidden by the bound feet of ignorance. This is the uncle I did not know, and could not know, and will never know. And though a single slender generation divides us, the civilizational gap between us reveals an abyss of loss. If the American Hebraists are in eclipse, it is because we, who might have been their successors (as the Puritans were their visionary precursors), have turned out to be incurious illiterates. Like some intelligent subspecies, we gaze at the letters—should we even recognize them for what they are—and cannot see their meaning.

Monsters

IN THE UNIVERSE OF CRITICS, ESSAYISTS, BIOG-
raphers, publishers, journalists, bloggers, and so on, only the
poets and a few chosen novelists are privileged to think of
themselves as monsters. When Rilke advises aspiring young
poets to "confess to yourself whether you would have to die
if writing were denied you," he is recommending poetry as a
kind of martyrdom, or the loss of it as a call to suicide. And
when Flaubert, observing an ordinary family enjoying a fine
afternoon, reflects, *"Ils sont dans le vrai"* — it is they who live
in reality — he is recognizing, perhaps wistfully, the condition
of the writer as a deformed outlier. "I detest my fellow beings," he once admitted, "and do not feel that I am their fellow at all." Seeming to fall into contradiction, Flaubert also
wrote in favor of the habits of the middling bourgeoisie: "Be
regular and orderly in your life," he said, "so that you may
be fierce and original in your work" — but this was plainly a
tribute to ferocity, not to regularity. Byron as England's literary bad boy; Tolstoy abandoning Sonya, his wife and lifelong
amanuensis; George Eliot, flouter of the received moral will;

the Beat poets, all of them stoned: generation after generation, the image of the writer's rebellious flight from the commonplace holds.

The writer as a figure apart, the writer as unfrocked monk — Tolstoy for the sake of ascetic godliness, Kafka for the sake of the enigma of guilt and punishment, Flaubert for the sake of *le mot juste,* Rilke for the sake of the most extreme of admonitions: *You must change your life.* But also: Keats and Blake and Wordsworth and the Beats and Emily Dickinson for the sake of exaltation. Put it that the Romantic era still whispers, and even old lost Dionysus distantly cries out. Rare is the writer who chooses to be seen as a proper citizen, though a few, like Thomas Mann or Henry James or John Cheever, will act out a long-lasting practiced façade — until time and happenstance come to reveal the furies below; or, as in *Death in Venice,* the writer himself discloses his hidden doppelgänger.

Yet apart from the fata morgana of fame, which bewitches nearly all beginning writers, biographers and critics are helpless to name the buried motive of any writer. Not that on occasion the thorn that spurs can't be readily evident — because it is scarcely buried at all: social grievance, for instance. Think of the strange trajectory of Tillie Olsen, who, while thwarted early on by what she felt to be the devouring constraints of motherhood and money, bravely wrote, even so, stories decrying those constraints — the most lauded of which is "Tell Me a Riddle," a blow against domesticity and custom. In 1962, when those former obligations were well in the past, and she was already acclaimed a feminist hero, she published *Silences,* her final work, a cri de coeur that addressed writing "aborted, deferred, denied." "I have had special need," she wrote, "to learn all I could of this over the years, myself so nearly remaining mute and having to let writing die over and over again in me." But rewarded afterward with close to five decades of personal freedom, affectionate celebrity, and public honors, she repeatedly lamented those old, unhappy, and (she emphasized) unjust times—and never again sat down to write anew. She lived to ninety-four.

Mostly, though, the secret engine that stirs into life a driven and unappeasable hunger to write cannot be prized out by assessing the writer's background or experience or temperament. Biography on the trail of clues is useless and misleading. What in E. M. Forster's life can account for the echo in the Marabar Caves? What in the complex narrative of Conrad's change of country and language can unriddle the origin of the secret sharer? Who can uncover the source of Malamud's Jewbird? Such signs and omens are the work of unnatural divination. The critic may parse and parse: a futility. Easy enough to find surface motivation in the psychologist's shelf of elixirs, those vials of reasonable cause and effect. But the writer's need is subterranean, unfathomable, subversive, and *O, reason not the need!*

Rabbi Leo Baeck, meanwhile, citing both Hegel and Kant, calls for reason as necessity, reason defined as "an essential part of that honesty man owes to himself: the test of criticism." Presumably he means self-criticism, the practice of restraint and moderation, the reserved and steady posture of the good citizen.

Monsters in their rapture elude such tests. They know

themselves to be visionaries carried off by some innate force to the fields of Arcadia, or else to the banks of Alph, the sacred river; or even, with Persephone, to a gloomy enchanted underworld. So much, then, for what can be glimpsed through the usual magic casements: let the poets be poets. But what of the sober-minded critics, who (see above) parse and parse, who are thinkers, exegetes, rationalists, close kin to historians and biographers, guardians and guarantors of humanism? The nearest that Samuel Johnson, the English-speaking world's most formidable critic, ever came to an expression of exaltation is his observation that "happiness consists in the multiplicity of agreeable consciousness." Such arithmetic weightiness, ringing with materialist authority though it may be, will never waken Orpheus.

A radically different authority, so rare as to be prodigious, is borne by a critic who, surprisingly, claims Dr. Johnson as precursor and mentor, and whose contemporary stature is not far from Johnsonian. He is, moreover, his own Boswell, taking note of his every thought and impulse, and when he utters "I," it is out of openness and intimacy:

> Samuel Johnson spoke of our "hunger of imagination," and conceded that Shakespeare alone assuaged that dangerous prevalence. Perhaps Shakespeare helped Johnson avoid madness, a function that has served for me whenever I waver in my own perilous balance.

Yet Harold Bloom ("so rare as to be prodigious" has already disclosed this critic's identity) wields another, even more powerful, key to his "I": the self that surrenders to the oracular, the self that willingly submits to submersion in ecstasy. Whatever it is that poets of the Orphic (or call it mystical) variety experience, Bloom too experiences, or longs to. In this he is like no other critic: why then, since he knows in his marrow what poets know, and long ago uncovered this knowledge as poets do, in childhood, is he not a poet? He tells us why he is not:

> I have been rereading *Moby-Dick* since I fell in love with the book in 1940, a boy of ten enthralled with Hart Crane, Whitman, William Blake, Shakespeare. *Moby-Dick* made a fifth with *The Bridge*, *Song of Myself*, Blake's *The Four Zoas*, and *King Lear*, a visionary company that transformed a changeling child into an exegetical enthusiast adept at appreciation rather than a poet. A superstitious soul, then and now, I feared being devoured by ravenous daemons if I crossed the line into creation.

Other little boys of ten, a few perhaps even destined to become critics themselves, were, in 1940, reading the Hardy Boys series, while little girls of ten with similarly conscious literary pinings were likely, in that era of innocent childhood, to be besotted with Jo March. But should anyone doubt that a word-struck child of ten can be susceptible to the exaltations of Hart Crane's image-mobbed lines, or that the boy Bloom was already a Childe Harold, a Byronic literary pilgrim "glimmering through the dream of things that were," then let such a doubter recall an earlier unearthly infant: John Stuart Mill, who, having been taught Greek at three, by the age of eight had mastered the *Anabasis,* all of Herodotus, the six dialogues of Plato, and much more. And Mill, like Bloom, never "crossed the line into creativity," at least not of the Xanadu kind. Erudition, however voluminous, is not poetry. Enthusiasm, however exultingly heart-stunned, is not poetry. But who would wish to exclude either the rationalist philosopher or the rhapsodic critic from the genus monster?

"A poet," Bloom writes of Whitman, "who equates his soul with the fourfold metaphor of night, death, the mother, and the sea is thinking figuratively as fiercely as did the Hermeticists and the Kabbalists." To this he adds poignantly, "At eighty-four, I lie awake at night, after a first sleep, and murmur Crane, Whitman, Shakespeare to myself, seeking comfort through continuity, as grand voices somehow hold off the permanent darkness that gathers though it does not fall." These are the yearning yet inflamed intimations not of a poet, but of a lover — a critic who has fallen in love with incantation as a conduit to the Elysian horizon luringly beyond his reach. And like any monster gazing past the rest of us, he stares alone.

Writers, Visible and Invisible

Writers' invisibility has little to do with Fame, just as Fame has little to do with Literature. (Fame merits its capital F for its fickleness, Literature its capital L for its lastingness.) Thespians, celebrities, and politicians, whose appetite for bottomless draughts of public acclaim, much of it manufactured, is beyond any normal measure, may feed hotly on Fame—but Fame is always a product of the present culture: topical and variable, hence ephemeral. Writers are made otherwise. What writers prize is simpler, quieter, and more enduring than clamorous Fame: it is recognition. Fame, by and large, is an accountant's category, tallied in amazonian sales. Recognition, hushed and inherent in the silence of the page, is a reader's category: its stealth is its wealth.

And recognition itself can be fragile, a light too easily shuttered. Recall Henry James's lamentation over his culminating New York Edition, with its considered revisions and invaluable prefaces: the mammoth work of a lifetime unheralded, unread, unsold. That all this came to be munificently reversed is of no moment: the denizens of Parnassus are deaf to after-the-fact earthly notice; belatedness does them no good. Nothing is more poisonous to steady recognition than death: how often is a writer — lauded, feted, bemedaled — plummeted into eclipse no more than a year or two after the final departure? Already Norman Mailer is a distant unregretted noise, and William Styron a mote in the middle distance (a phrase the nearly forgotten Max Beerbohm applied to the fading Henry James). As for poor befuddled mystical Jack Kerouac and declamatory fiddle-strumming mystical Allen Ginsberg, both are diminished to Documents of an Era: the stale turf of social historians and excitable professors of cultural studies.

Yet these eruptions of sudden mufflings and posthumous silences must be ranked entirely apart from the forced muteness of living writers who work in minority languages, away from the klieg lights of the lingua franca, and whose oeuvres linger too often untranslated. The invisibility of recently dead writers is one thing, and can even, in certain cases (I would be pleased to name a few), bring relief; but the invisibility of the living is a different matter altogether, crucial to literary continuity. Political shunning — of writers who are made invisible, and also inaudible, by repressive design — results in what might be called *public* invisibility, rooted in external circumstance: the thuggish prejudices of gangsters who run rotted regimes, the vengeful prejudices of corrupt academics who propose intellectual boycotts, the shallow prejudices of the publishing lords of the currently dominant languages, and finally (reductio ad absurdum!) the ideologically narrow prejudices of some magazine editors. All these are rampant and scandalous and undermining. But what of an intrinsic, delicate, and far more ubiquitous *private* invisibility?

Vladimir Nabokov was once an invisible writer suffering from three of these unhappy conditions: the public, the private, the linguistic. As an émigré fleeing the Bolshevik upheavals, and later as a refugee from the Nazis, he escaped the twentieth century's two great tyrannies. And as an émigré writing in Russian in Berlin and Paris, he remained invisible to nearly all but his exiled compatriots. Only on his arrival in America did the marginalizing term "émigré" begin to vanish, replaced first by the notion of citizen, and ultimately by American writer—since it was in America that the invisible became invincible. But Brian Boyd, in *Nabokov: The American Years,* his intimate yet panoramic biography, recounts the difficulty of invisible ink turning visible—not only in the protracted struggle for the publication of *Lolita,* but in the most liberal of literary journals. It was the otherwise audacious *New Yorker* of the 1950s that rejected a chapter of *Pnin,* the novel chronicling Nabokov's helplessly charming and self-parodying alter ego, "because," according to Boyd, "Nabokov refused to remove references—all historically accurate—to the regime of Lenin and Stalin." (The phrases in question included "medieval tortures in a Soviet jail," "Bolshevik dictatorship," and "hopeless injustice," characterizations that the editors apparently regarded either as excessive or as outright falsehoods.) Certainly the politically expelled chapter did not languish in invisibility for very long; and as for *Lolita,* decades after its electrifying and enduring triumph, it burst out once again, dazzlingly, in the title of Azar Nafisi's widely admired memoir linking Lolita's fate to the ruthless mullahs of Tehran. (Still, even today, even in New York, one can find a distinguished liberal journal willing to make a political pariah of a writer: an instance of ordinarily visible ink rendered punitively invisible.)

And here at last is the crux and the paradox: writers are hidden beings. You have never met one — or, if you should ever believe you are seeing a writer, or having an argument with a writer, or listening to a talk by a writer, then you can be sure it is all a mistake. Inevitably, we are returned to Henry James, who long ago unriddled the conundrum of writers' invisibility. In a story called "The Private Life," Clare Vawdrey, a writer burdened by one of those peculiar Jamesian names (rhyming perhaps not accidentally with "tawdry"), is visible everywhere in every conceivable social situation. He is always available for a conversation or a stroll, always accessible, always pleasantly anecdotal, never remote or preoccupied. He has a light-minded bourgeois affability: "He talks, he circulates," James's narrator informs us, "he's awfully popular, he flirts with you." His work, as it happens, is the very opposite of his visible character: it is steeped in unalloyed greatness. One evening, while Vawdrey is loitering outdoors on a terrace, exchanging banalities with a companion, the narrator steals into Vawdrey's room — only to discover him seated at his writing table in the dark, feverishly driving his pen. Since it is physically impossible for a material body to be in two places simultaneously, the narrator concludes that the social Vawdrey is a phantom, while the writer working in the dark is the real Vawdrey. "One is the genius," he explains, "the other's the bourgeois, and it's only the bourgeois whom we personally know."

And lest we dismiss this as merely another of James's ghost stories, or simply as a comical parable, we had better recall that celebrated Jamesian credo, a declaration of private panic mixed with prayerful intuition, which so many writers secretly keep tacked over their desks: "We work in the dark — we do what we can — we give what we have. Our doubt is our passion, and our passion is our task." The statement ends memorably, "The rest is the madness of art."

The madness of art? Maybe so. But more likely it is the logic of invisibility. James has it backwards. It's not the social personality who is the ghost; it is the writer with shoulders bent over paper, the hazy simulacrum whom we will never personally know, the wraith who hides out in the dark while her palpable effigy walks abroad, talking and circulating and sometimes even flirting. Sightings of these ghost writers are rare and few and unreliable, but there is extant a small accumulation of paranormal glimpses that can guide us, at least a little, to a proper taxonomy. For instance: this blustering, arrogant, self-assured, muscularly disdainful writer who belittles and brushes you aside, what is he really? When illicitly spotted facing the lonely glow of his computer screen, he is no more than a frightened milquetoast paralyzed by the prospect of having to begin a new sentence. And that apologetically obsequious, self-effacing, breathlessly diffident and deprecatory creature turns out, when in the trance-like grip of nocturnal ardor, to be a fiery furnace of unopposable authority and galloping certainty. Writers are what they genuinely are only when they are at work in the silent and instinctual cell of ghostly solitude, and never when they are out industriously chatting on the terrace.

What is the true meaning of "the madness of art"? Imposture, impersonation, fakery, make-believe — but not the imposture, impersonation, fakery, or transporting make-believe of inventive storytelling. No: rather, art turns mad in pursuit of the false face of wishful distraction. The fraudulent writer is the visible one, the crowd-seeker, the crowd-speaker, the one who will go out to dinner with you with a motive in mind, or will stand and talk at you, or will discuss mutual writing habits with you, or will gossip with you about other novelists and their enviable good luck or their gratifying bad luck. The fraudulent writer is like Bellow's Henderson: *I want, I want, I want.*

If all this is so—and it *is* so—then how might a young would-be writer aspire to join the company of the passionately ghostly invisibles? Or, to put it another way, though all writers are now and again unavoidably compelled to become visible, how to maintain a coveted clandestine authentic invisibility? Don't all young writers look to the precincts of visibility, where heated phalanxes of worn old writers march back and forth, fanning their brows with their favorable reviews? Isn't that how it's done, via models and mentors and the wise counsel of seasoned editors? "I beg you," says Rilke, addressing one such young writer,

> I beg you to give all that up. You are looking outwards, and of all things that is what you must now not do. Nobody can advise you and help you, nobody. There is only one single means. Go inside yourself. Discover the motive that bids you to write; examine whether it sends its roots down to the deepest places in your heart, confess to yourself whether you would have to die if writing were denied you. This before all: ask yourself in the quietest hour of the night: *must* I write? Dig down into yourself for a deep answer. And if this should be in the affirmative, if

you may meet this solemn question with a strong and simple "*I must,*" then build your life according to this necessity.

Thus the poet Rilke, imploring the untried young to surrender all worldly reward, including the spur, and sometimes the romantic delusion, of Fame, in order to succumb to a career in ectoplasm. Note that he speaks of "the quietest hour of the night," which is also the darkest, where we do what we can and give what we have. The madness of art — and again I willingly contradict Henry James — is not in the art, but in the madding and maddening crowd, where all manner of visibilities elbow one another, while the ghosts at their writing tables sit alone and write, and write, and write, as if the necessary transparency of their souls depended upon it.

Out from Xanadu

In my late teens and early twenties I was a mystic. It was Blake and Shelley who induced those grand intoxications, and also Keats and Wordsworth and Coleridge. At New York University, where Thomas Wolfe had once taught freshman composition, his shade — *O lost, and by the wind grieved, ghost, come back again* — sometimes still flickered. Dylan Thomas, not yet in his cups and not yet renowned, came to a handful of students in an ordinary classroom and chanted, as if to a hall of hundreds, *The force that through the green fuse drives the flower,* syllables instinct with divine afflatus. Meanwhile I was writing an undergraduate thesis on the Romantic poets, and though I knew neither the word nor the concept, I was at that time seriously antinomian. Nothing was distinct, or of its own indivisible nature, nothing was fixed, nothing was demanded: all was wavering spirit and intuition. Rapture and ecstasy, ecstasy and rapture! — these were imagination's transports, abetted by the piercing sweetness of melancholy. The sage was withered from the lake, and no birds sang; or else they chorused thrillingly, like celestial choirs.

Besides being a mystic and an antinomian, I was also a believing monist: all things were one thing, watercolor worlds leaching and blending and fading into porous malleable realms. Yearning and beauty were the heart's engines, shocking the waiting soul (mine, anyhow) into a pulsing blur of wonderment. In Xanadu, where Alph, the sacred river, ran, you might actually see the blessed damozel leaning out from the golden bar of Heaven! As for where the Spirit of God dwelled . . . well, where else but in you and me? (Primarily, of course, in me.) The Ten Commandments? In Xanadu nobody had ever heard of them.

At twenty-four I blundered, I no longer recall where or how, into "Romantic Religion," a trenchant meditation — or manifesto, or scholarly credo — by Leo Baeck. His name, his stature, his personal history, his transcendent learning, were all unfamiliar. That he was of that remarkable German-Jewish generation which included, among many other humanist eminences, the historian Gershom Scholem and the philosophers Martin Buber and Walter Benjamin, I had yet to discover. Nor did I know that Baeck was a rabbi consumed, beyond the vastnesses of his own multifaceted tradition, by Greek and Christian thought; or that he was of that minute fraction of Jewish humanity to have come out of Theresienstadt alive. When I stumbled into the majesties of "Romantic Religion," I was as one (so it seemed to me afterward) who had conversed with Socrates while ignorant of Socrates' origins and identity.

Not that Baeck was Socratic in his tone or approach. His essay was a formidable looking glass. In a dissenting voice more analytic than scornful (though scorn seethed behind it), he told me off. For the romantic, he wrote, "everything dissolves into feeling; everything becomes mere mood; everything becomes subjective. . . . Fervently, the romantic enjoys the highest delight and the deepest pain day after day; he enjoys the most enchanting and the most sublime; he enjoys his wounds and the streaming blood of his heart. . . . Experiences with their many echoes and billows stand higher in his estimation than life with its tasks; for tasks always establish a bond with harsh reality. And from this he is in flight. He does not want to wrestle for his blessing, but to experience it, abandoning himself, devoid of will, to what spells salvation and bliss." And again: "Everything, thinking and poetry, knowledge and illusion, all here and all above, flows together in a foaming poem, into a sacred music, into a great transfiguration, an apotheosis. In the end, the floods close over the soul, while all and nothing become one."

In the hundred energetic pages of Walter Kaufmann's translation from the German (Kaufmann was himself a Princeton philosopher), under headings such as "Ethics," "Humanity," and "The Sentimental," Rabbi Baeck had me dead to rights. I had been surrendering my youth to *Weltschmerz,* to *Schwärmerei,* to *Welttrunkenheit,* all those unleashed Wagnerian emotions which, Baeck pointed out, Hegel had once dismissed as the displacement of "content and substance" by "a formless weaving of the spirit within itself." The opposite of all that besottedness was "the classical, ethical idea of history" as manifested in "the Kantian personality who confronts us as the bearer of the moral law" — the law of act and deed that is itself "an essential part of that honesty which man owes to himself: the test of criticism." Who could criticize a dream? And what was that dream but immersion in fantasy and illusion? "Ethics evaporates into exaltation," Baeck declaimed. "Justice is to be reduced to a mere feeling and experience; the good deed is effected not by human will but by divine grace; man himself is a mere object and not a personality. The will becomes supernatural, and only concupiscence remains to man. . . . Something more diametrically opposed to ethics than romanticism would be hard to find."

And reading on and on in a fever of introspection, I was beginning to undergo a curious transformation: not the spirit's visionary turning, but one willed and chosen. I had become the Ancient Mariner — only in reverse. Gazing down at the water snakes writhing below, Coleridge's mystical sailor is all at once seized by a burst of joyous sanctification: to his transfigured senses the repulsive creatures of the sea are now revealed as blessèd things of beauty. But I, pursuing passage after passage of Baeck's reprise of the incantatory romantic — its transports and exultations, its voluptuously nurtured sorrows, its illusory beauty anchored in nothing but vapor — I came to see it all as loathsome, no different from those mindlessly coiling water snakes. What did it lead to? The self. What did it mean? Self-pride. What did it achieve? Self-delusion and delirium. That way lay Dionysus. I chose Rabbi Baeck.

More decades than I wish to admit to have fled away since I first looked into "Romantic Religion." And just recently, when I revisited my old copy — battered from many coerced lendings (it was I who did the coercing), and almost always returned unread — I was still impressed by its bold intellectual and moral cogency. But its power seemed somehow diminished, or, if not exactly that, then a tiny bit stale. I had, after all, assimilated those ideas from multiple sources over the years (not counting the Bible), and by now they were locked, as we have learned to say, into my DNA. "Romantic Religion," with its emphasis on humane conduct over the perils of the loosened imagination, remains an essay to live by. It is not an essay to write stories by; stories crave the wilderness of untethered feeling. But once — even though I wanted then more than anything on earth to write stories — it left me dazzled and undone.

The Rhapsodist

This rounded, wet, weedy, windy earth, with its opposing poles, was born into contraries: Apollo and Dionysus, Talmudist and Kabbalist, sober exegete and rapt ecstatic. Harold Bloom, who bestrides our literary world like a willfully idiosyncratic Colossus, belongs to the party of rapture. He is himself no Whitman or Melville, no Emily Dickinson or Robert Frost or Wallace Stevens; no Hart Crane or Emerson. And yet he seems at times almost as large as any of these, so vital and particularized is his presence. If, as Emerson claims, the true ship is the shipbuilder, then is the true poem the critic who maps and parses and inhabits it? Can poet and critic be equal seers?

Read Bloom, and you may be led to suppose it so. "Walt Whitman," he writes, "overwhelms me, possesses me, as only a few others — Dante, Shakespeare, Milton — consistently flood my entire being. . . . Without vision, criticism perishes." And: "I rejoice at all strong transports of sublimity." And again: "True criticism recognizes itself as a form of memoir." And finally, emphatically: "I believe there is no critical method except yourself." It is through intoxicating impulses such as these that Bloom has come to his formulation of the American Sublime, and from this to his revelation of the daemon: the very Higgs boson of the sublime. Bloom's beguiling daemon can be construed as the god-within; he is sire to the exaltations of apotheosis, shamanism, Gnosticism, Orphism, Hermeticism, and, closer to home, Emerson's "Self-Reliance." He is made manifest through the voices of poets and in the chants of those weavers of tales, like Melville and Faulkner, who are kin to poets.

The Daemon Knows, the enigmatic title of Bloom's newest work of oracular criticism, is strangely intransitive. What is it that the daemon knows? We are meant to understand that the daemon is an incarnation of an intuition beyond ordinary apperception, and that this knowing lies in the halo of feeling that glows out of the language of poetry. "To ask the question of the daemon is to seek an origin of inspiration," Bloom instructs, and his teacherly aim is to pose the question in close readings of twelve daemon-possessed writers whom he interrogates in pairs: Whitman with Melville, Emerson with Dickinson, Hawthorne with Henry James, Mark Twain with Frost, Stevens with T. S. Eliot, Faulkner with Hart Crane. He might well have chosen twelve others, he tells us, reciting still another blizzard of American luminaries, but dismisses the possibility "because these [chosen] writers represent our incessant effort to transcend the human without forsaking humanism." (A question Bloom does not put — we will approach it shortly — is whether shamanism, Orphism, Gnosticism, Hermeticism, and all the other mystical isms, including the idea of the daemon, do in fact cling to humanism.)

For Bloom, the origin of inspiration is dual: the daemon that ignites it from within, and the genealogical force that pursues it from without. The bloodline infusion of literary precursors has long been a leitmotif for Bloom, from the academic implosion of *The Anxiety of Influence* more than forty years ago to the more recent *The Anatomy of Influence*. Here he invokes the primacy of Emerson as germinating ancestor:

> For me, Emerson is the fountain of the American will to know the self and its drive for sublimity. The American poets who (to me) matter the most are all Emersonians of one kind or another: Walt Whitman, Emily Dickinson, Edwin Arlington Robinson, Robert Frost, Wallace Stevens, Hart Crane, John Ashbery, A. R. Ammons, Elizabeth Bishop, May Swenson, Henri Cole. Our greatest creators of prose fiction were not Emersonians, yet the protagonists of Hawthorne, Melville, and Henry James frequently are beyond our understanding if we do not see Hester Prynne, Captain Ahab, and Isabel Archer as self-reliant questers.

Though Bloom's persuasive family trees are many-branched, the power of influential predecessors nevertheless stands apart from daemonic possession. According to Bloom, the daemon — "pure energy, free of morality" — is far more intrinsic than thematic affinity. However aggressively their passions invade, it is not Whitman alone who gives birth to Melville, or Emerson to Dickinson, or Hawthorne to James, or Mark Twain to Frost; and certainly it is not the lurid Faulkner, all on his own, who rivals the clay that will become Hart Crane. Literary heritage is half; the rest is the daemon. "*Moby-Dick*," Bloom sums up, "is at the center of this American heretical scripture, our worship of the god-within, which pragmatically means of the daemon who knows how it is done." But there is yet another pragmatic demonstration to be urged and elaborated. "Hart Crane's daemon," he adds, "knows how it is done and creates an epic of Pindaric odes, lyrics, meditations, and supernal longings without precedent."

Without precedent: surely this is the earliest key, in Bloom's scheme, to the daemon's magickings. Theme and tone and voice may have authorial ancestors; what we call inspiration has none. Turning to one of his two commanding touchstones (the other is Whitman), Bloom cites Emerson: "This is that which the strong genius works upon: the region of destiny, of aspiration, of the unknown. . . . For the best part, I repeat, of any life is not that which he knows, but that which hovers in gleams, suggestions, tantalizing unpossessed before him." So when Bloom tells us that there can be no critical method other than the critic himself—meaning Bloom—we should not take it as blowhard hyperbole. With Emerson, he intends to pry open the unpossessed and to possess it, and to lead the reader to possess it too: a critical principle rooted in ampleness and generosity.

In this way, the illustrative excerpts Bloom selects from the work of his hallowed dozen are more than concentrated wine tastings; they are libraries in little. In considering Hawthorne, he discusses—in full—"Wakefield" and "Feathertop," two lesser-known stories, as well as *The Blithedale Romance, The Marble Faun,* and the canonical *The Scarlet Letter* and *The House of the Seven Gables.* In his discant on James, Bloom supplies entire scenes from *The Portrait of a Lady, The Bostonians,* and *The Wings of the Dove,* in addition to long passages of "The Jolly Corner." And in crisscrossing from Hawthorne to James and back again, he leaves nothing and no one unconnected. "Where indeed in American fiction," he asks, "could there be a woman loftier, purer, as beautiful and as wise as Hester Prynne? Isabel Archer is the only likely candidate," though he goes on to lament her choice of the "odious Osmond." For Bloom, Moby-Dick consorts with Huck Finn, and Emily Dickinson with Shakespeare, while Whitman underlies, or agitates, Stevens, Hart Crane, and, surprisingly, T. S. Eliot.

Of all Bloom's couplings, Stevens and Eliot are the oddest and the crankiest. Despite the unexpected common link with Whitman, the juxtaposition is puzzling. Bloom's veneration of Stevens, sometimes "moved almost to tears," is unfailing. "From start to end, his work is a solar litany. . . . He has helped me to live my life," he confesses. Yet nearly in the same breath Bloom is overt, even irascible, in his distaste for Eliot, partly in repudiation of "his virulent anti-Semitism, in the age of Hitler's death camps," but also because of his clericalism: "Is it my personal prejudice only that finds no aesthetic value whatever in the devotional verse of T. S. Eliot? . . . He brings out the worst in me. His dogmatism, dislike of women, debasement of ordinary human existence make me furious." In the same dismissive vein, he disposes of Ezra Pound: "I at last weary of his sprawl and squalor." Nowhere else in this celebratory volume can such a tone — of anger and disgust — be found. Not even in Bloom's dispute with what he zealously dubs "the School of Resentment" (the politicization of literary studies) is he so vehement as here.

Still, emotive disclosures are not foreign to this critic's temperament. He has, after all, already told us that criticism can be a form of memoir. "I am an experiential and personalizing literary critic," he explains, "which certainly rouses up enmity, but I go on believing that poems matter only if we matter." Out of this credo grows a confiding intimacy: "The obscure being

I could call Bloom's daemon has known how it is done, and I have not. His true name (has he one?) I cannot discover, but I am grateful to him for teaching the classes, writing the books, enduring the mishaps and illnesses, and nurturing the fictions of continuity that sustain my eighty-fifth year." A touching reminder of the nature of the human quotidian, its riches and its vicissitudes, its successes and its losses: tangled mortal life itself, pulsing onward in the daylight world of reality. But is this what Bloom's exalted twelve have taught of how the daemon, that rhapsodic creature of "pure energy, free of morality," is purposed? The daemon who is trance, who is the mystical whiteness of the white whale, who is harp and altar of Hart Crane's bridge, and who enters solely into seers and poets? Can the daemon's lover — who is Bloom — harbor the daemon in himself? Or, to put it otherwise: may the professor of poetry don the poet's mantle?

Meanwhile, the daemon knows, and Bloom knows too, who are his most dedicated antagonists. They are those verifiable humanists, the rabbis who repudiate the Kabbalists, who refute the seductions of Orphists and Gnostics, who deny the dervishing god-within and linger still in that perilous garden, birthplace of the moral edict and the sober deed, where mortals dare to eat of the Tree of the Knowledge of Good and Evil, and daemons of the sublime are passing incantatory delusions.

And there are no poets.

Souls

ONE OF THE MOST QUOTED COMMENTS OF THE twentieth century—Theodor Adorno's "To write poetry after Auschwitz is barbaric"—has lost its relevance, if not its force, and is now obsolete. This stringently cautionary sentence derives from "Cultural Criticism and Society," the essay in which it is embedded, together with a still more caustic remark: "Even the most extreme consciousness of doom threatens to degenerate into idle chatter." Does poetry, then, equate to idle chatter? And to extend these notions further: after Auschwitz, do the multifaceted realms of literature, including the novel, all boil down to idle chatter?

However Adorno, the formidable German-Jewish philosopher of aesthetics, might have regarded such a proposition, it is not as outrageous as it may sound on first hearing. Adorno set down this dictum in 1949, when the ovens had scarcely cooled, and the now entrenched "Holocaust," in its uniquely capitalized meaning, had not yet been established—partly because for a long time no single naming could sufficiently encompass it. The legal term "genocide," coined in 1946 by Raphael Lemkin, a Polish-Jewish lawyer — forty-seven members of whose family were murdered — was ignited in the crucible of the German depredations, but is nowadays more broadly intended. Paul Celan, the Romanian-Jewish poet who survived only to drown himself afterward, avoided any representation or characterization, settling, with acid anonymity, on "that which happened."

But whether that-which-happened is named or not named, the events themselves have failed to be quarantined. The abysmal sadism symbolized by the two sparse syllables of "Auschwitz" should, by its savagery, silence every pen — though even now, habituated as we are to an infinity of images of Nazi inhumanity, both actual and imagined, we still cannot fathom the full nature of what we have come to call the Holocaust. And no pen, for good or ill, has been silenced: Adorno's pronouncement has been ten thousand times defied, dismissed, and finally undone. Literature, history, memoir, biography, film, theater, opera, painting, philosophical meditation, psychological speculation, sociological analysis — whatever the approach, all proliferate oceanically. The farther the Holocaust recedes from us, the more is written and sung and dramatized. Even one of the most searing of Holocaust poems, "Written in Pencil in a Sealed Boxcar," by Dan Pagis — an Israeli poet who himself endured three years in Transnistria — must, in representing the unspeakable, submit to utterance, however broken:

> *Here in this transport*
> *I am Eve*
> *with my son Abel*

if you see my elder son
Cain son of Adam
tell him that I

And here it is necessary to look again at Adorno's declaration—not the phrase that is his most renowned, but the one far less so, though perhaps more crucially telling: *Even the most extreme consciousness of doom threatens to degenerate into idle chatter.* Barbaric cruelty is, for its victims, merciless yet finite—a shooting, a hanging, a hacking, a gassing, a rocketing, a bombing, a beheading. But idle chatter leaves an endless cultural trail, and worse, it crushes into trivia whatever it fingers. Horror too can turn into careless trivia. When history is abused, it becomes no better than the gossip of the lie; it influences what we believe.

But what of fiction, what of the novel, what of the mighty rush of imagination that is reputed to render truth by other means? Do the rights of history preclude, or even erase, the rights of fiction? This is a question in perpetual motion, a question that never dies, and some years ago I was moved to invoke it yet again:

On what basis can one disdain a story that subverts document and archive? On what basis can one protest a novel that falsifies memory? If fiction annihilates fact, that is the imagination's prerogative. If fiction evades plausibility, that too is the imagination's prerogative. Fiction has license to do anything it pleases. Fiction is liberty at its purest. Why should the make-believe people in novels be obliged to concur with history, or confirm it? Characters in fiction are not illustrations or representations. They are freely imagined fabrications; they have nothing to do with the living or the dead; they go their own way. Is the novelist to be compelled to honor typicality? Or faulted for choosing what is atypical? The novelist is neither sociologist, nor journalist, nor demographer. Imagination owes nothing to what we call reality; it owes nothing to history. The phrase "historical novel" is mainly an oxymoron. And there the matter ends.

Or does it? Why, then, do we recoil from comic inventions that spoof the perpetrators of the Holocaust? Or from improbable Holocaust scenes and themes? Why does satire of the Holocaust—acrid wit, the enemy of the fool and the knave—nevertheless make us uneasy? Perhaps for this reason: what is permissible to the playfully ingenious author of *Robinson Crusoe*—fiction masking as chronicle, the implausible pretending authority—is not permitted to those who touch on the uprooting and obliteration of six million Jewish lives, and the extirpation of their millennial civilization in Europe. The Roman playwright Terence said it first and fastest: *Aliis si licet, tibi non licet*—what others may do, you may not do. To laugh at the funny little man with the funny little mustache and the frenzied gesticulations gives the funny little man the last laugh: it is he who successfully lived out his heinous dream of mass gassings.

The novel is not, after all, a sealed jar. As much as it is the product of culture, it also alters culture by its implicit criticism of manners, motives, and beliefs: only think of Gatsby, Frank Alpine, Dorothea Casaubon, Gilbert Osmond, Raskolnikov, Bartleby, Kurtz. The novel can educate the heart—

meaning the enlargement of its sympathies—or it can deceptively shrink those sympathies. (As in E. M. Forster's *The Longest Journey,* wherein a woman usurps her fiancé's integrity simply by uttering "we." A scene of such subtlety that one may be led to suppose it a demonstration of the unity of love.)

And a "Holocaust novel," so called, has the power to corrupt history, and thereby the reader's heart, by its contradiction of what is actual and factual: Bernhard Schlink's *The Reader,* for instance, a widely praised fable that exonerates an Auschwitz SS guard by reason of her illiteracy (she was innocent of what she was signing up for)—and this in a society boasting, at the time, Europe's loftiest literacy rate. In *Alice in Wonderland,* say, or *The Hobbit,* the fictive imagination is the handmaiden of delightful implausibility. In a Holocaust novel, imagination's implausibility can turn out to be the henchman of lie; and then the guileless reader, more tabula rasa than scholar, will fall prey to mistaking the illusory for the reasonably credible. Worse yet, it can sometimes happen (*vide* Martin Amis) that the writer's unassailably honorable and feelingful intent—to expose outright human wickedness—is subverted by imagination's wandering lure.

Even more perilous is the most evocative device of language: metaphor. Is there any distance between the Nazis' characterization of Jews as "vermin" and the use of Zyklon B, a common household insecticide, to suffocate Jews in sealed cages? In metaphor's most notorious incarnation, it adopts the definite article: "the Jew," to which any appalling attribute may be attached. Metaphor is also closely connected to imposture, one thing masking as a dissimilar thing in order either to enhance perception ("rosy-fingered dawn") or to darken it. Consider, though warily, William Gass's *Middle C,* a novel premised in part on the notion of imposture, where "Jew" stands as an emblem of both universal victim and universal deceiver. Gass's purely metaphorical Jews conjure a vision of uncanny rites and costumes, and of a clannish cabal devoted to vindictive excommunication: nightmarish scenes made stranger yet by the circumstance that these prevaricating "Jews" are in reality Austrian Gentiles pretending to be Jews. Is a hate-mocking irony at work here, irony as still another instance of metaphor's protean guises? Doubtless: its images, nevertheless, are unhappily drawn from the anciently familiar poisoned well of "the Jew." And to mock is not always to dispel.

When Celan chose not to name the unspeakable, this too was a kind of mockery, though a profoundly and intimately painful one, acknowledging the absence of a merciful protector-God during one of the most deliberately barbarous periods of human history. Judaism in its uncompromising monotheism is careful not to depict God, either in image or word, lest the naming of God lead to a description of what is deemed to be beyond human envisioning or understanding. Yet the overwhelming human need to name cannot be resisted, and is, in fact, divinely mandated: recall that the God of Genesis gave to Adam, the First Human, the task of naming everything he saw, bestowing a cognitive value on plant and animal and earth and stone and sky and water. But did this privilege apply also to naming Adam's thoughts, and might the Thought of God have been one of those thoughts? The Bible does not say, so it is a paradox — a double paradox — that what may have been given to Adam is withheld from his progeny: any utterance of the unutterable name of God. When Moses appeals to God to speak His name, the reply is the mysteriously nameless Tetragrammaton: *I am that which I am.* Hence the second paradox: that the least avoided and most common God-utterance in Jewish practice is not, as one would expect, the Nameless One, but simply *ha-Shem,* the Name.

Celan, then, was being bitterly and blasphemously and mockingly unforgiving in his refusal to give a name to the the atrocities of the camps — because *ha-Shem* by His silence had so betrayed His people that the immaculate namelessness which honors the sanctity of God Celan would confer also on the foulest evil of the murderers. Or so he may be read, evidenced by "Death-fugue," the most piercing of his poems. Its baleful refrain, *der Tod ist ein Meister aus Deutschland* — Death is a Master from Germany — displaces the cosmically sublime Hebrew liturgical phrase "Master of the Universe" (*melekh ha-olam*). Here among the chimneys the Master of the Universe, banished by jackboots, no longer speaks nor rules nor shelters nor saves; it is Death, coming out of its lair in Germany, who is Master. And where names are usurped or erased, numbers will suffice: the tattoos on the arms and wrists of the doomed.

But what of the names that are known, and understood, and fathomed to the dregs, yet are purposefully denied utterance? Like the poets Pagis and Celan, the historian, philosopher, sociologist, and novelist H. G. Adler was among the tattooed, and though left alive, was irreparably marked by both Theresienstadt and Auschwitz. A native of Prague, he fled the Soviet oppression that followed the German defeat and escaped to London, where, in addition to massively conceived scholarly work, he completed his Holocaust trilogy: partly autobiographical, partly metaphorical. Here—in Adler—is no American writer, reared in peaceable safety, imagining false Jews running away from the imminent German annexation of Austria; and here is no British writer, similarly reared in peaceable safety, imagining the private lives of SS officials and their families. Whatever it may mean to have "experienced" Theresienstadt, whatever it may mean to have "survived" Auschwitz, it is a knowledge that Adler possesses in the marrow of his bones. And like Celan, like Pagis, he will not utter outright the name of that knowledge. In the vastly suffering scope of *The Wall,* the third volume of Adler's trilogy, the bodily wails of dread and desolation are metaphorized as an ever-lurking wall. A symbol. An image.

Peter Filkins, Adler's American translator, notes in his introduction to *The Journey,* the first of the three related novels, that nowhere in Adler's fiction "are the words *Nazi, Hitler, Germans, Jews, camps, gas chambers, ghetto,* et cetera, ever used." He reminds the reader that "Adler and Adorno corresponded, and it was on this position that they came to deep disagreement. Adler believed it not only possible to write poetry and literature after Auschwitz but that it was necessary, for only with the full engagement of the imagination would it be possible to elicit even a glimmer of the true nature of what had been suffered and, yes, survived. . . . In this way," Filkins continues, "Adler's work is about Theresienstadt and not about it at the same time." And in this way metaphor (or metonymy, as Adler has it) can become the enemy of memory; also the enemy of history, or memory-made-retrievable. Jews living or dead are not Everyman. They are not symbols. They are not the means of art, and when they are the object of the imagination, they can sometimes end in peril. ("Vermin.") They live and they die, like all other human beings, in their individuated and particularized historical explicitness. It may be that in a time to come, and in the absence of the explicit, Pagis's "sealed freightcar" will merely puzzle; Celan's *Meister aus Deutschland,"* with its tropes of music and dance and vipers, may be thought to be a choirmaster or a choreographer or even a zookeeper; and Adler's impassioned yet abstracted trilogy will have dissolved into that flattened commonplace: man's inhumanity to man.

When narratives are sham, when namelessness suffices and metaphor clouds, then what is left if not Adorno's idle chatter?

"I Write Because I Hate": William Gass

Of all living literary figures, William Gass may count as the most daringly scathing and the most assertively fecund: in language, in ideas, in intricacy of form (essays zigzagging thought); above all in relentless fury. "I write because I hate," he declaimed in a 1977 *Paris Review* interview. And to a French journalist, decades on: "I wish to indict mankind." A Swiftian project: Gass's plenitude of evils swarms named and naked in *Middle C*, a novel prodigal in deceits and impostures. From its opening notes until its coda, this unquiet Bildungsroman is designed to detonate its mild and middling title. Even more telling, the crooked limbs of its deceptions pass, as if heritable, from father to son.

The father is Rudi Skizzen, an Austrian born in Graz, a changeable man who can play a merry fiddle. Conscious of the spreading stain in his native country even before the Anschluss and Vienna's jubilant welcome to Hitler, he departs with his family for England, not as a dissenting Austrian but as a fleeing Jew. In London he is reinvented as Yankel Fixel, an *Opfer*, a victim ("Jew" reduced to foggy metaphor), and compels his unwilling wife and children to take on what he imagines to be Jewish custom, costume, and uneasy repute. It is a brief and clumsy phase, made harsher by the depredations of the Blitz, and cut short by a phantasmagorical row of black-hatted accusers, baleful Elders of Zion who "denounce" the false Jew. Better to morph into a spotless Englishman, so Rudi's next impersonation is as Raymond Scofield, a janitor who wins big at the track, abandons his family, and vanishes out of the narrative. Motiveless and unexplained.

He leaves behind for young Joey, his London-born son, a malignant legacy: Joey will become, like his father, a liar. The lie is integral to his very name, Skizzen, the plural of the German for "sketch" — quick improvisation, the liar's tool. (Listen also for the echo of schism, schizoid, even scissors, the split into doubleness and duplicity. Gass's nomenclature delves deeper than any Dickensian whimsy.) Nor did the lie leave Joey and his mother and sister when the lying paterfamilias left. Still pretending to be pitiable Jewish refugees, they hoodwink a bureaucratic path to America, and come to rest in Ohio, where they can throw off their reluctant disguise and grow, if they wish, into middle Americans. Joey's sister succeeds in her quest for the ordinary, while his mother, remembering the flowery fields of her home village, sets out to dig a humble garden, tossing unwanted worms into a coffee can.

But Joey harbors the ghost of his father's fiddle, and is drawn inescapably to a battered old upright found in the street, and to Mr. Hirk, a music teacher with crippled hands who tutors him in scales and the mastery of "Indian Love Call." In time he ascends beyond Mr. Hirk, from the simple to the sublime, leaping the rungs from Beethoven to the pinnacle of Schönberg. He takes a job in a record store, where he is permitted the use of the piano, and where, though innocent, he is charged with theft, and learns what it is to feel helpless before injustice; yet he steals packets of seeds for his mother. He begins to read thirstily, inexorably. He attends a Lutheran college devoted to narrow piety (which doesn't prevent a French teacher's attempt to seduce him), and is excoriated for sectarian disloyalty; he has been playing the organ in a Catholic church. Though he has come into the country illicitly and has no Social Security identification, he finds work and a kind of friendship in a public library, where his own amateur forgery of a driver's license is perfected by a skilled preservationist.

In all these plot-rich incidents, and in scores more, Gass appears to be a straightforward sympathetic psychological storyteller, despite a hovering nimbus of things awry; of flaw and fraud. But soon enough a wilderness intrudes: the tender and aspiring young Joey, immersed in books and music, living with his mother after his sister has gone off to marry a potato farmer, is revealed to be an obsessive, a secret prevaricator who will always be living with his mother. In middle-C Ohio he is a *diabolus in musica*, a discordant and anomalous note. What seizes Joseph Skizzen (who will become Professor Skizzen, Whittlebauer College's published and respected professor of music), what claws at his brain, are the pullulations of all the world's evils. Indefatigably, he collects newspaper clippings of global catastrophes, from tribal animosities to sex crimes and genital deformations, from HIV and Holocaust atrocities and the burning of the Library of Alexandria to mudslides and tornadoes and capsized ferries. Taint and trauma and torment. His scissors is his rake, and he heaps up these jumbles of horror in what he calls his Inhumanity Museum. He sees how pain and wickedness fructify, even as his mother's increasing skills proliferate into the busy contradictions of a garden teeming with blooms and larval infestation. He is like the man in the fairy tale whose sight is so powerful that he must bind his eyes with a blindfold lest he see too unbearably much: every droplet on every leaf, every particle of foam in every sea, every wound in every heart; only Joseph Skizzen's eyes are unbound, and every drop is shed blood.

Nor is this the whole of his obsession. Growing parallel with his museum of cuttings, Skizzen's forgeries, and his misgivings, multiply. His academic credentials, his college degree and his doctorate, and his music studies in Vienna are all fakes and inventions. Like his father before him, he seems to be what he is not. And his unrelenting aim is to crush into a single sentence God's crucial query over the fate of the cities of the plain — ought humanity, so inhumane, to endure? An elusive sentence, which he works over and over again, shaping and reshaping it, until it can fit, just so, and under the sign of Schönberg, into twelve spare words.

Gass's sentences are, happily, not so succinct, and they are most exhilaratingly ingenious when they venture into unexpected and dizzying keys, diving from vernacular directness into an atonal Niagaran deluge: so many ironies, so many propositions, so many juxtapositions, so many interleaved passages of youth and maturity, so many ripe monologues and mazy musings, so many catalogues and refrains, so many instances of horrific calamity, so many digressions (they all finally stream into Gass's oceanic scheme). What are we to make of this world-devouring novel, and of the title that is its warning sentry? Ought we to believe Skizzen when he claims that "his lifelong ruse ... was the equivalent of Moses's tablets before they got inscribed:

a person pure, clean, undefiled, unspoiled by the terrible history of the earth"? That the leveling of middle-C mediocrity can be an escape from becoming an agent of evil? That middle C offers the quasi-innocence of the bystander?

Or is the concept of the Inhumanity Museum itself defiled, not simply by the filth of its contents, but by its inherent intent? An indiscriminate welter of wrongs and ordeals levels all woe; it lacks the hierarchy of purposefulness. Is there to be no moral calculation applied to the sources of suffering, no asking who ordered it, or why? Is drowning by tsunami equal to suffocation in a gas chamber? Or overgrazing to germ warfare? In Skizzen's muddled museum, nature and man are equal offenders, unranked evil is everywhere middling, happenstance and massacre stand cheek by jowl in chorus, there can be no worse or worser. Then under the sway of random equivalence, who will presume to indict, and how can one not wonder whether Skizzen's museum might be Gass's too?

Love and Levity at Auschwitz: Martin Amis

She was coming back from the Old Town with her two daughters, and they were already well within the Zone of Interest. Up ahead, waiting to receive them stretched an avenue — almost a colonnade — of maples, their branches and lobed leaves interlocking overhead. A late afternoon in midsummer, with minutely glinting midges. . . . Tall, broad, and full, and yet light of foot, in a crenellated white ankle-length dress and a cream-colored straw hat with a black band, and swinging a straw bag (the girls, also in white, had the straw hats and the straw bags), she moved in and out of pockets of fuzzy, fawny, leonine warmth. She laughed — head back, with tautened neck.

So begins "First Sight," the opening chapter of *The Zone of Interest*, Martin Amis's provocatively titled fourteenth novel — but where, then, are we really? The Old Town, after all, might be anywhere in the old world of romantic allusiveness. *A late afternoon in midsummer:* isn't that where we first discover Isabel Archer, yet another enchanting figure seen within a verdant vista? Or might this radiant painterly vision — the white dress, the dappled path, the insouciant tread — reflect Leonard Woolf's rapturous first glimpse of Virginia Stephen, also in white dress and round hat, "as when in a picture gallery you suddenly come face to face with a great Rembrandt or Velasquez"?

As for the Zone of Interest, this too can be found anywhere, including the erotic turf of the psyche — and isn't instant infatuation frequently fiction's particular zone of interest? Here, though, the phrase will shock a knowing ear — it is, in its original German, the *Interessengebiet* of a sprawling Third Reich death camp: an area cleared of its native residents to accommodate workaday camp administration, storage for gas cylinders, barracks for the lesser SS, and housing for the officers and their families. The laughing, light-footed young woman who so quickly captivates the narrator is Frau Hannah Doll, the wife of Kommandant Paul Doll, the man chiefly responsible for the efficient running of the murder factory. And Golo Thomsen, her love-struck observer, is himself an officer charged with slave labor operations at the adjacent I. G. Farben Buna-Werke. It is he who will argue over how much brute hunger a slave worker can endure before he grows useless and is shot or sent to the gas. He also has the distinction of being the nephew of Martin Bormann, Hitler's private secretary, confidant, and trusted deputy.

The leafy idyll, it turns out, is a sham, the artful novelist's Potemkin village masking rot. Hence the publisher's absurdist blast: *love in a concentration camp.* And love, moreover, not among the sexless doomed, but in the privileged quarters of the masters of death — yet another upstairs-downstairs drama, upstairs as usual plush and advantaged and lavishly expressive of feeling; downstairs a hill of skulls. *Anus mundi* as viewed not by the broken and the damned, but by their shatterers. A satire, then? A bitter comedy?

By now, seventy years after the closing of the camps, *The Zone of Interest*, however else it is perceived, must be regarded as a historical novel, a literary convention by its nature inexorably tethered to verifiable events. All the same, it remains a novel, with fiction's primal freedom to invent its own happenings, both the plausible and the implausible, the sympathetic along with the repellent, the antic embedded in the unspeakable. Imagination is sovereign. Characters are at liberty to contemplate their lives and shape and assess them as they wish. Interior thought is rampant. We are privy to all things hidden: rivalry, vanity, deception, jealousy, lust.

Scripture, which purports to be history, is mainly impatient with interiority. It is God, we are told, who hardens Pharaoh's heart, and after this no more need be said. Pharaoh's wickedness is absolute, dyed in the marrow, opaque; no light can be leached from it. We are not permitted to know more than the intractable breadth and depth of this wickedness — nothing of Pharaoh's psychology, nothing of his inner musings, nothing of his everyday, how he was appareled, whether he was sometimes tipsy, or if he bantered with his courtiers, how often he summoned women of the palace, or of the brickworks, to his bed; or if he ever faltered in remorse. God is a judge, not a novelist; this is the meaning of a God-hardened heart: the deed's the thing.

Novelists, mini-gods though they may be, do not harden hearts, and inner musings are their métier. A deed, however foul, has an origin, or call it a backstory, and every backstory is a kind of explanation, and every explanation is on its way to becoming, if not quite an absolution, then certainly a diagnosis. And then the evildoer (if such an absolutist term is admissible), having been palpated for diagnosis, is reduced from zealous criminal to one possessed of a "condition" not of his own making—insanity, perhaps, or the inevitable outcome of an ideological rearing. In literary fiction (here we naturally exclude comic strips and melodrama) there are no outright villains, and even a pharaoh would be interestingly introspective.

In an afterword both bibliographical and discursive—itself an anomaly in a novel—Amis grapples with the monstrous question of such explanatory mitigations: monstrous because it teeters perilously over the filthy chasm of exculpation. In support of the novelist's right to imagine the inmost workings of evil's agents, he cites, reverently, a passage from Primo Levi:

> Perhaps one cannot, what is more one must not, understand what happened, because to understand is almost to justify. Let me explain: "understanding" a proposal or human behavior means to "contain" it, contain its author, put oneself in his place, identify with him. Now no normal person will ever be able to identify with Hitler, Himmler, Goebbels, Eichmann, and endless others. This dismays us, and at the same time gives us a sense of relief, because perhaps it is desirable that their words (and also, unfortunately, their deeds) cannot be comprehensible to us. They are non-human words and deeds, really counter-human.... There is no rationality in Nazi hatred; it is a hate that is not in us; it is outside man.

A hate that is outside man. It would appear on the face of it that Levi's insight is nothing if not instinctively biblical: hearts so hardened, and deeds so inhumanly wicked, that only God can fathom them. Yet Amis comes away from these seemingly transparent reflections with the sense of having been granted permission, or even a blessing. "Historians," he begins, "will consider this more an evasion than an argument," and goes on to remind us that Levi was also a novelist and a poet, placing him "very far from hoisting up the no-entry sign demanded by the sphinxists, the anti-explainers." Instead, Amis oddly insists (against Levi's plain language) that it is Levi himself who is "pointing a way in."

And Amis's way in to the hate that is outside man is fully and unstintingly the novelist's way. If the deed's the thing, it's not the only thing. Soliloquies that tunnel into minds to expose their folly or their intransigence or their delusions, and sometimes their disillusions. The permutations of plot, the rise and fall of ambition and hope, whether in the rivalrous bureaucracy of death-making or in the chancy living and automated dying of the doomed. And of course the tentative strivings of the well-advertised *love in a concentration camp*. The camp is, after all, a hierarchical society; a kind of village, a veritable *Middlemarch* of Nazidom; or better yet, given its dense though highly transient population, a bustling, busy city with recurring traffic bottlenecks, especially at the ramp, where the selections take place. In cinematic mode, there are scenes outdoors and indoors. Outdoors: always the ramp looming over its thickened plaza of human detritus, the *Stücke* ("pieces," as one speaks of inanimate cargo) just disgorged from the freight cars; and the tragic Szmul, the most pitiable of the doomed, the grieving overseer of a vast heaving meadow of human ash, a *Sonderkommando* fated to escort the unsuspecting victims to their end.

And indoors: The SS bigwigs and their wives at the theater (the *Interessengebiet* is not without *Kultur*), or enjoying a concert, or a ballet where the young principal dancer is one of the *Häftlinge.* Ilse Grese, a sadistic and lecherous female guard seen in her private billet—her surname that of a notorious SS *Helferin* tried after the war and hanged for savagery, her Christian name invoking Ilse Koch of human-skin lampshade infamy. Martin Bormann at home *en famille*, his wife Gerda perpetually and aspiringly pregnant (each of her nine surviving children named for yet another prominent Nazi), hoping to receive a coveted award for Aryan fertility. The charming villa of Paul and Hannah Doll, with its garden and pet tortoise, its *Häftling* Polish gardener, a former professor of zoology, and its *Häftling* housemaid, a compliant Jehovah's Witness suitably called Humilia. The pampered Doll daughters, cosseted in the routines of a normal childhood (their mother duly accompanies them to school and sees to their proper bedtime), perturbed by their sickly pony, brokenhearted over the killing of their tortoise, yet oblivious to the hourly killing all around. The unfortunate Alisz, widow of a German soldier, herself only recently welcome at the dinner table, now a subhuman confined in a solitary cell, tainted by the discovery of her Sinti (Gypsy) blood. And pervasively, both indoors and out: the relentlessly inescapable smell of burning human flesh.

"My own inner narrative," Amis notes, "is one of chronic stasis. . . . I first read Martin Gilbert's *The Holocaust: the Jewish Tragedy* in 1987; in 2011 I read it again, and my incredulity was intact and entire—it was wholly undiminished." The phrase "chronic stasis," even removed from the intent of its context and on its own, is remarkable for what it imparts. *The Zone of*

Interest is not Amis's first venture into the deadly morass of assembly-line Jew-killing. It was preceded two decades earlier by *Time's Arrow,* an Ezekiel-inspired vision of reversed chronology: the bony dead refreshed into bloom. Clearly, Amis is possessed by these smoldering particulars; he is not among those worldly sick-and-tired-of-hearing-about-it casuists for whom the Holocaust has gone stale to the point of insult. In a novel so hotly close to the rind of history, he is scrupulously faithful to the findings of the scholars and committed to a flawless representation of place, time, and event. Most telling is his admission of a single purposeful deviation: "My only conscious liberty with the factual record was in bringing forward the defection to the USSR of Friedrich Paulus (the losing commander at Stalingrad) by about seven months." The confession attests to the novelist's aversion to manipulative fakery.

The facts, accordingly, are meticulously attended to; but then, as mockery follows mockery, come the voices with their slyly revealing ironies that turn self-deception into satire, and self-appraisal into stinging disclosure. Kommandant Doll is frequently the butt of these unwitting sallies, as when, contemplating his personal nature, he declares himself "a normal man with normal feelings. When I'm tempted by human weakness, however, I simply think of Germany and of the trust reposed in me by her Deliverer, whose visions, whose ideals and aspirations, I unshakably share." And here Amis may be lampooning Hannah Arendt's inflammatory thesis of the "banality" of a murderous SS zealot — as if he were to ask, what could be more commonplace, more *normal,* than full-bore fanaticism?

But ridicule finds a still ampler berth: Doll, questioning

Prufer, his second-in-command and "an unimpeachable Nazi,"
is eager to learn how the siege of Stalingrad is proceeding.

"Oh, we'll carry the day, mein Kommandant," he said over
lunch in the Officers' Mess. "The German soldier scoffs at the
objective conditions."

"Yes, but what *are* the objective conditions?"

"Well we're outnumbered. On paper. Ach, any German is
worth 5 Russians. We have the fanaticism and the will. They
can't match us for merciless brutality."

"... Are you sure about that, Prufer?" I asked. "Very stubborn resistance." ...

"With our zeal? Victory's not in doubt. It'll just take a little
longer."

"I hear we're undersupplied. There are shortages."

"True. There's hardly any fuel. Or food. They're eating the
horses."

"And the cats, I heard."

"They finished the cats."

The absurdity builds: dysentery, lice, frostbite, dwindling
ammunition, encirclement; and finally surrender. And still the
clownish back-and-forth of illusory confidence: "The German
ranks are impregnable." "Besides, privation presents no problem to the men of the Wehrmacht." "For a German soldier, these
difficulties are nothing." "How can we go down to a rabble of
Jews and peasants? *Don't* make me laugh."

A pair of buffoons. Abbott and Costello in Nazi dress.

Doll, meanwhile, is regarded as an incompetent fool even by

his confederates. His peroration on the ramp—following the usual reassuring litany of disinfection, showers, hot soup afterward—is a failure, since it introduces what is instantly suspect: *"But if there's anything you especially treasure and can't afford to be without, then pop it in the barrel at the end of the ramp."* "You don't deceive them any more," they chide him. ". . . There are some very unpleasant scenes nearly every time. . . . You sound so insincere. As if you don't believe it yourself." To which Doll indignantly responds, "Well, of course I don't believe it myself. . . . How could I? You think I'm off my head?"

Arendt, so proudly sealed in intellect that nothing could penetrate the armor of her synthesis, ended less in condemnation than in mitigation—her neutered Eichmann is a weak-kneed pharaoh, scarcely worth all those plagues. History as comedy has a parallel effect: it trivializes the unconscionable. The blood the clown spills is always ketchup.

Hannah Doll is not trivialized. She baits her husband, she withholds sex, she listens to subversive enemy radio; and, as we eventually discover, she has privately given the Kommandant a black eye. To hide the shame of it, he pins the blame on the Polish *Häftling* and his shovel. And to add to the gardener's fabricated culpability, it is Doll himself who smashes the tortoise so prized by his young daughters. As penalty, his hapless victim is swiftly dispatched to his death. Throughout all this grim chaos, Amis means us to view Hannah as an internal dissident, a melancholy prisoner of circumstance: perhaps even as a highly privileged quasi-*Häftling* powerless to rebel. Though seeing through Doll's cowardice and deception, she conforms, however grumblingly, to bourgeois life among the chimneys— the dinners, the playgoing, the children's indulgences. Her own indulgence: cigarettes, the lesser reek intended to overcome the greater. Her open derision, seen by Doll's colleagues as a wifely nuisance, is pointless; the fake showerheads continue to spew their poison. Her needling humiliations of Doll affect nothing; the daily business of the ramp prevails.

In the historic facticity of the camps, does Hannah Doll have a real-life counterpart? And does it matter if she does or doesn't? The women of the camps have left a substantial record, not only the grisly SS *Helferinnen* with their uniforms and whips, but the SS wives in their well-appointed villas, shamelessly flaunting rings and necklaces seized from the doomed. The base activities of many such women are documented in Wendy Lower's *Hitler's Furies: German Women in the Nazi Killing Fields,* a volume not included among Amis's acknowledgments — though Hannah is proof of his copious knowledge of these spousal miscreants: she is their purposefully contrapuntal projection.

"What is especially striking about these wives," Lower writes, "is that . . . they were not officially given any direct role in the division of labor that made the Holocaust possible. Yet their proximity to the murderers and their own ideological fanaticism made many of them into potential participants." She instances Erna Petri, the wife of Horst Petri — an SS officer attached to the Race and Settlement Office (a euphemism for the mass annihilation of Jews) — who found cowering at a roadside six half-naked little boys somehow escaped from a death-bound freight car. She took them home, fed them, and then, one by one, shot each child in the back of the neck. Liesel Willhaus, another SS wife and a crack shot, delighted in picking off Jews from her balcony. SS honeymooners celebrated their love in the midst of deportations and mass executions. All in all, exemplars of SS wives reveling in atrocities abound — and still this heinous chronicle yields not a single Hannah Doll.

Golo Thomsen, Hannah's aspiring lover, is made of the same exceptionalism. From his position defending slow starvation of the Buna slave laborers — against a proposal that a few more daily calories would speed the work — he at length comes to welcome Germany's defeat. So much so that, calling on the little English he can muster, he quietly joins a British prisoner of war in reciting "Rule Britannia" — even as he recognizes that the man is a likely Buna saboteur. (As it happens, not an ounce of the synthetic rubber vaunted by the Germans ever emerged from the Buna-Werke.) That an SS official, the nephew of Martin Bormann, a Nazi of such elevated rank that he dines with the Führer at his gilded mountain retreat, should end as a turncoat in the harshest hour of Germany's eastern Blitzkrieg . . . ah, but isn't this the very conundrum woven by the twining of history and fiction? Has a believably disaffected Golo Thomsen ever been known to recant in an actual Zone of Interest? Do the oceanic testimonies of this fraught period throw up any evidence of even one SS officer who, while within earshot of the cries of the doomed, decried those cries? And if not, it must be asked again: does it matter?

History commands communal representation — nations, movements, the reigning Zeitgeist. Fiction champions the individuated figure. Bovary is Bovary, not an insubstantiation of the overall nature of the French bourgeoisie. Characters in novels (unless those novels are meant to be allegories) are no one but themselves, not stand-ins or symbols of societies or populations. History is ineluctably bound to the authenticity of documents; but all things are permitted to fiction, however contradictory it may be of the known record. It is this freedom to posit redemptive phantoms that justifies the historic anomalies that are Hannah Doll and Golo Thomsen. And further: no literary framework is more liberated from obligation to the claims of history than comedy, with its manifold jesters: parody, satire, farce, caricature, pratfall. All these are entertainments — and so it is that we are frankly entertained by Kommandant Doll, even as he stands "with sturdy fists planted on jodhpured hips" on the murderous ramp. And still further: something there is in the resistance to parody that is obtuse, dense, dully unread. What of Gulliver, what of Quixote? To resist the legacy of their majestic makers is to deny literature itself. Then why resist Amis, their daringly obsessed if lesser colleague? And why pursue skepticism of *love in a concentration camp*? Or of latecomer dissidents who nevertheless eat and drink in comfort on the lip of the merciless inferno?

Read beforehand, as one is tempted to do, Amis's afterword becomes the novel's mentor and conscience. In it he echoes Paul Celan's "coldly muted" naming of the Holocaust as "that which happened" — a phrase again reminiscent of the biblical refusal of elaboration — and adds, "I am reminded of W. G. Sebald's dry aside to the effect that no serious person ever thinks of anything else." In this way the afterword, in combination with *Sonderkommando* Szmul, the novel's third interior voice, repudiates and virtually annuls all other voices, the farcical with the ahistorical; and nearly erases also the dominating voice of the novel itself. For Szmul, no suspension of disbelief, fiction's busy handmaiden, is required, and no element of caricature can touch him. He alone is immune to the reader's skepticism, he alone is safe from even the possibility of diminishment through parody; and this holds both within the novel's pliancy and in the tougher arena of historical truth.

It is Szmul who speaks of "the *extraterritorial* nature of the Lager": "I feel we are dealing with propositions and alternatives that have never been discussed before, have never needed to be discussed before—I feel that if you knew every minute, every hour, every day of history, you would find no exemplum, no model, no precedent." His macabre task ("the detail," as he obliquely calls it) is to shepherd the doomed to the gas, and then to dispose of their close-packed corpses first to the ovens, and then to the limitless and undulating fields of ash. As a secret-bearing witness, he will soon be consumed by the very fire that he himself facilitated:

> When squads of heavily armed men come to the crematoria and this or that section of the detail knows that it is time, the chosen Sonders take their leave with a nod or a word or a wave of the hand—or not even that. They take their leave with their eyes on the floor. And later, when I say Kaddish for the departed, they are already forgotten.

Szmul is one of the chosen—chosen by the power of the jackboot to be the servant of these gruesome rites. Ruth Franklin, reviewing the novel in the *New York Times*, describes the "crematory ravens" of the *Sonderkommando* as "the nadir of degradation," "a portrait of depravity." But Amis's Szmul is a presence of lacerating pathos and unrelenting mourning. In a brittle tone so colloquially matter-of-fact as to shatter its burden, he ruminates, "I used to have the greatest respect for nightmares—for their intelligence and artistry. Now I think nightmares are pathetic. They are quite incapable of coming up with anything as remotely terrible as what I do all day." He recalls a time at Chelmno when the quantities of carcasses were so overwhelming that the SS "selected another hundred Jews to help the Sonders drag the bodies to the mass grave. This supplementary Kommando consisted of teenage boys. They were given no food or water, and they worked for twelve hours under the lash, naked in the snow and the petrified mud." Szmul's two sons were among them; and in this plainspoken account we can perhaps hear (yet only if we are open to it) a judgment on the omnipresent misuse and abuse of "that which happened." Amis's crematory raven flies out from the novel as its single invincibly convincing voice.

Despite the afterword's dismissal of "the sphinxists, the anti-explainers," it is they, knowing what is at stake, who are finally in the right. And what is at stake is the conviction that premeditated and cocksure evil is its own representation, sealed and sufficient. A hardened heart needs no reason beyond its own opacity. The ripened deed is all; to riff on it is to veil it. This is not to say that *The Zone of Interest* ought never to have departed the wilder precincts of Amis's cunning imaginings. It is good to have this fractious novel. It makes the best argument against itself.

An Empty Coffin:
H. G. Adler

Of Homer we know nothing, of Jane Austen not enough, of Kafka more and more, sometimes hour by hour; and yet Achilles and Elizabeth Bennet and Joseph K press imperially on, independent of their makers. Lasting works hardly require us to be acquainted with the lives of the masters who bore them — they have pulsing hearts of their own. Still, on occasion there emerges a tale that refuses to let go of its teller, that is unwilling, even in the name of art, to break free; or cannot. This is less a question of autobiographical influence or persuasion than of an uncanny attachment: call it a haunting, the relentlessly obsessive permeation of a book by its author. Or imagine a man condemned for the rest of his days to carry, and care for, and inconsolably preserve his own umbilical cord.

In this way *The Wall*, the final novel of an exilic trilogy by H. G. (Hans Günther) Adler, is inseparable from the lacerating fortunes of the writer's life; the chronicle he gave birth to continues to claim him. It matters, then, that Adler was reared in a linguistically fraught Prague, and that like Kafka before him, he was a Jew steeped culturally in German within a society vigorously Czech. At Charles University he studied musicology, but as poet, scholar, historian, philosopher with a theological bent, and novelist above all, he subsequently encompassed far more. On February 8, 1942, three years after Germany's invasion of Czechoslovakia, he and his family were, as we have learned to say, deported — a Nazi palliative, with its elevated aura of Napoleon on Elba, for violent criminal abduction. He endured two and a half years in Theresienstadt, and in 1944 was sent by freight car to Auschwitz, where his physician wife and her mother were promptly gassed. His parents and sixteen relatives were similarly dispatched. Liberated in 1945, Adler returned to Prague, only to find it under rigid Soviet influence. In 1947 he escaped to London, where, buffeted by the forlorn displacements of a melancholic exile, he nevertheless completed a comprehensive and searingly definitive sociological study of Theresienstadt.

Arthur Landau, the voice and central consciousness of *The Wall*, traces a nearly identical trajectory, but so powerfully and strangely transfigured as to drive history into unsettling phantasmagoria. Names and habitations are veiled: Prague is "over there," London is "the metropolis," Jews go unmentioned, Germans and their deathly devisings the same; yet grief and terror and wounding memory beat on, unappeased. And meanwhile, in his modest new household in an unprepossessing neighborhood of the metropolis, where he lives quietly with Johanna, his sympathetic second wife, and their two children, Landau is laboring over an immense work of historiography, *The Sociology of Oppressed People.* He turns for support to an earlier wave of refugees from "over there," who by now are well situated either in business or as an established intellectual cohort. At first, remembering old friendships, they rally round him with bright promises of funding, then fail to follow through, until finally he is rawly rebuffed. The scholars disdain his ideas. The entrepreneurs scoff at his elitist impracticality, and offer inferior jobs in wallpaper and artificial pearls. "Unfortunately," he reflects, "it was too late for me. The time for refugees was past; they had all attached themselves to something or someone, and there was nothing left for foreigners. . . . I soon appreciated that there was one too many people in the world, and that was me. I simply couldn't be allowed to exist."

Existence, often as straightforwardly spoken as here, but more frequently mournfully eloquent, is the great clamor that tolls through the undulating passages of this wild-hearted novel. "I have ceased to exist," Landau laments, "called it quits, am completely spent, the vestige of a memory of who I no longer am. . . . I never even rise to the level of a dubious existence, the fragile bearing of a single nature, because I am homeless in every sense, belonging nowhere, therefore expendable, never missed." And again, in the voice of God to Adam: "You have eaten of the fruit; that cannot be undone. Your mistake is this: that you wish to exist; what's more, that you have done so from the very beginning and forevermore. You concern yourself much too intensely with that. Your will to be is inexhaustible."

The will to be becomes manifest in grotesque scenes and gargoyle-like figures thrown up by intimations of an elusive history of atrocity. And always an insinuating image, in the guise of a wall, stalks and oppresses Landau, now representing the unremitting ache of exile and loss, now the anguished past (although no more than a single paragraph in more than six hundred pages hints at the explicit reality of Auschwitz). Steadily encroaching, the wall is sometimes almost palpable, sometimes hidden. Even when it is absent, its influence is tormentingly theatrical, as when a pair of pallbearers come with a hearse to take Landau to be cremated. He refuses to go, though Johanna, out of courtesy, urges it, while politely inviting the pallbearers to eat dinner with the family beforehand. When the two return at a later time, promising a trip to a sociological conference, Landau agrees to sit uncomfortably on top of the empty coffin while Johanna and the children follow the hearse in a neighbor's vegetable truck. The conference turns out to be a street fair organized in honor of Landau himself, where all his old scorners and adversaries are selling tickets to the booths and bumper cars.

So it is that fantasy alternates with panic, and panic with sardonic realism. How to classify a work so circuitously and exhaustively structured? Adler's prose is tidal, surge after narrative surge rushing forward and then enigmatically receding, the moment displaced by memory, and memory by introspective soliloquy. In Peter Filkins's patiently loyal rendering, all these movements of telling and withdrawal are joined by smaller eddyings in the form of participle clauses that coat Adler's serpentine sentences with a Germanic otherness. The translator, or his publisher, has also appended a dramatis personae accompanied by a chapter-by-chapter summary. Rather than a help, these additions are a disservice, as if this majestic novel could not breathe on its own.

But it does breathe, and with a secret knowledge of untrammeled capacities. Adler has the courage of his idiosyncratic art, and though *The Wall* has been acclaimed a modernist masterwork, it is perversely premodern in its lavish freedom to go whither it will, and to ponder, and to linger, and to suffer felt experience to the lees. The ruined scenes of "over there" are visited again and again, the ghosts together with the remnant of the living. Landau, returned to his native city, searches for his father's shop and finds desolation. The apparitions who are his parents (his mother is seen sewing his shroud) shun him and drive him off. His old teacher, turning on him, reports him to the authorities. He toils in a museum of the doomed, collecting the cherished properties of a vanished population: paintings of family members, masses of abandoned prayer books. He is warmly befriended by Anna, the sister of a schoolmate who, like so many others, has not returned. Wandering with Anna along once familiar mountain trails, he remembers earlier excursions with the lost wife of his youth. And then the nervous flight across the border to attain, finally, the foreign metropolis. All this in disregard of sequential chronology; instead, time's elastic wooing, Now melting into Then, Then devouring Now.

In his richly authoritative introduction, Filkins refers to *The Wall* and the two novels that precede it, *The Journey* and *Panorama,* as Adler's Shoah trilogy. "However," he notes, "what is often most missing . . . is particulars." And here is a poignant conundrum. Fifty years on, encountering a narrative frame made purposefully abstract, where cities go nameless and horrors are loosened from their history, who will have the means to recognize Landau's wall for what it is? Or, at so increased a distance from the Europe of the last century, will Adler's universe, lacking in identifiable specificity (Theresienstadt, Auschwitz, Nuremberg Laws, Wehrmacht, SS, abductions, gassings, shootings, refugees, survivors), have fallen by then into piteous yet anodyne myth? A name is in itself a concrete history; namelessness is erasure. Even so universalized an image as hell has a name. It is called hell.